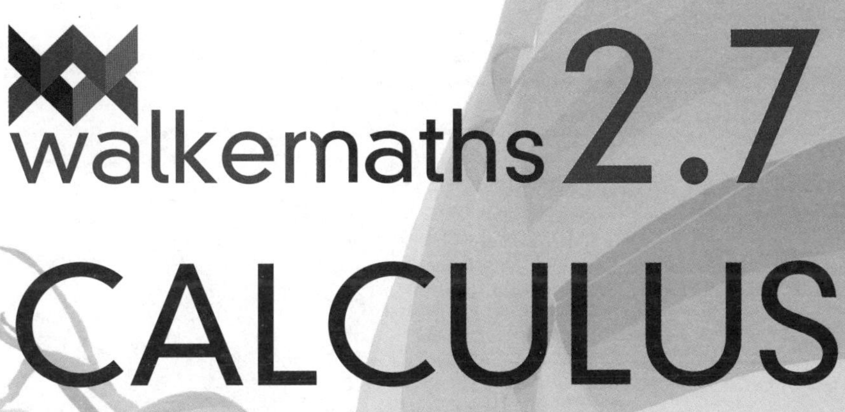

walkermaths 2.7

CALCULUS

NCEA Level 2 External

Charlotte Walker and Victoria Walker

Walker Maths 2.7 Calculus
1st Edition
Charlotte Walker Victoria Walker

Editor: Eva Chan
Cover and text design: Cheryl Smith, Macarn Design
Production controller: Siew Han Ong

Any URLs contained in this publication were checked for currency during the production process. Note, however, that the publisher cannot vouch for the ongoing currency of URLs.

Acknowledgements
Cover photo courtesy of Shutterstock.

We wish to thank the Boards of Trustees of Darfield and Riccarton High Schools for allowing us to use materials and ideas developed while teaching. Our thanks also go to all past and present colleagues who have generously shared their expertise and ideas.

For product information and technology assistance,
in Australia call **1300 790 853**;
in New Zealand call **0800 449 725**

For permission to use material from this text or product, please email
aust.permissions@cengage.com

National Library of New Zealand Cataloguing-in-Publication Data
A catalogue record for this book is available from the National Library of New Zealand.

ISBN 978 017 0 354233

Cengage Learning Australia
Level 7, 80 Dorcas Street
South Melbourne, Victoria, Australia 3205

For learning solutions, visit **cengage.com.au**

Printed in China by 1010 Printing International Limited
12 25

CONTENTS

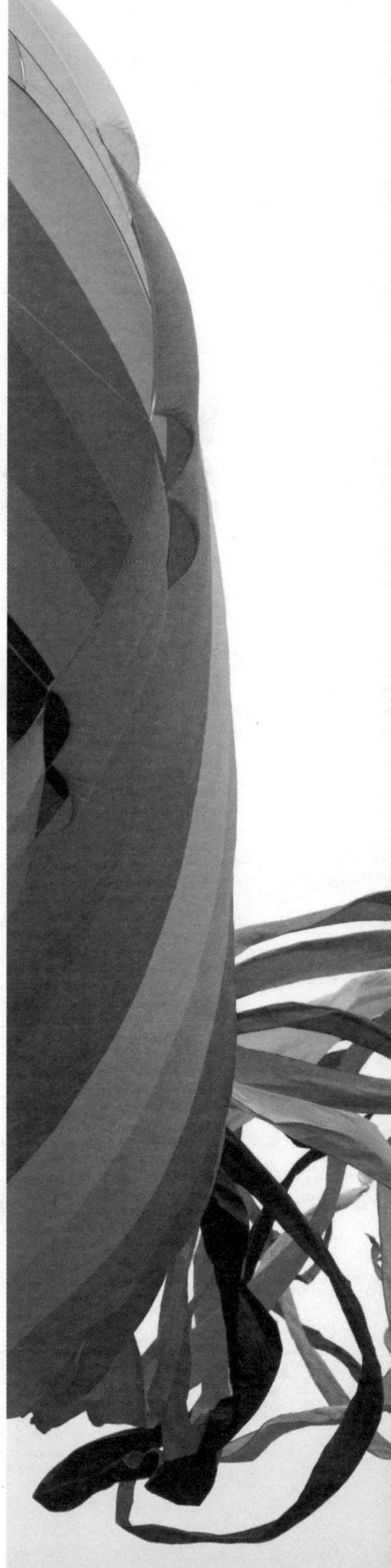

ISBN: 9780170354233

Formulae

These are the calculus formulae which are supplied in the external examination.

Differentiation	$\frac{d}{dx}(x^n) = nx^{n-1}$
Anti-differentiation	If $f'(x) = x^n$, then $f(x) = \frac{x^{n+1}}{n+1} + c$

Glossary

Make your own glossary of key terms:

Term	Definition	Picture/Example
Coefficient		
Exponent		
Constant		
Origin		
Differentiation		

  ISBN: 9780170354233

Term	Definition	Picture/Example
Anti-differentiation		
Integration		
Optimisation		
Maximum (plural: maxima)		
Minimum (plural: minima)		
Polynomial		
Constant of integration		
Parameters		
Kinematics		
Velocity		
Acceleration		

ISBN: 9780170354233

Introduction

Gradient revision

The gradient is the steepness, or slope, of a line.

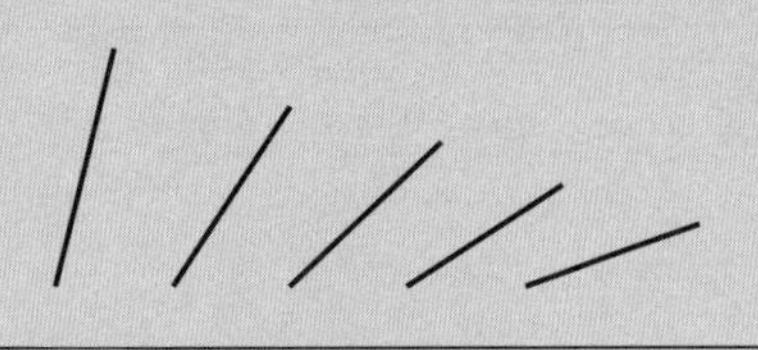

These lines all have positive gradients.

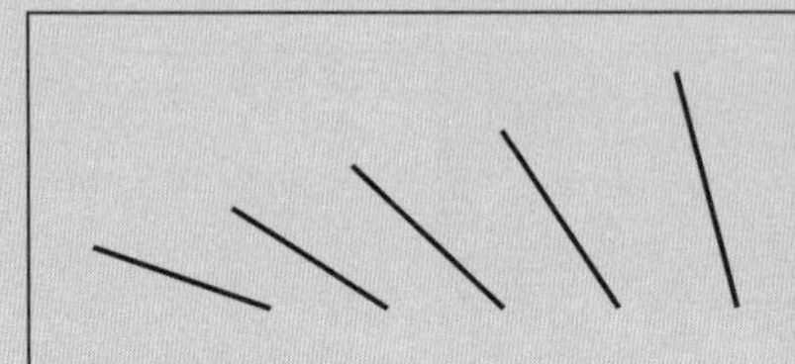

These lines all have negative gradients.

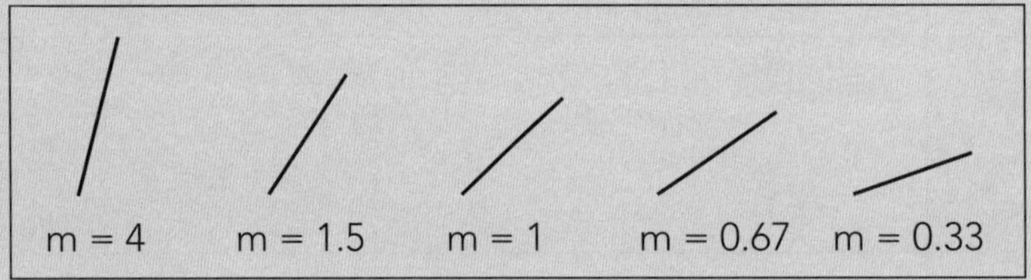

The steeper the line, the bigger the gradient.

The gradient is calculated using the formula $m = \frac{\text{change in } y}{\text{change in } x}$ or $\frac{\text{rise}}{\text{run}}$.

The easiest way to do this is to draw a right-angled triangle on the line.

$m = \frac{\text{rise}}{\text{run}}$

$= \frac{5}{6}$

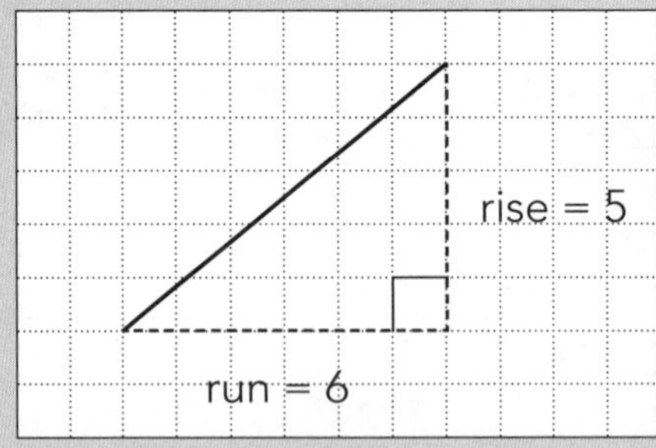

This time the gradient is *negative*.

$m = -\frac{\text{rise}}{\text{run}}$

$= -\frac{3}{7}$

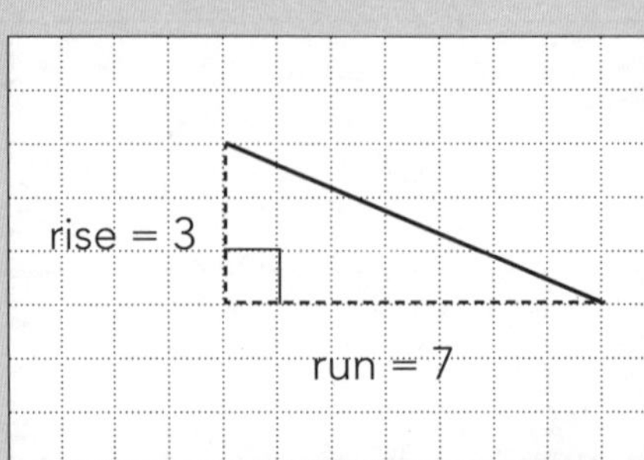

 ISBN: 9780170354233

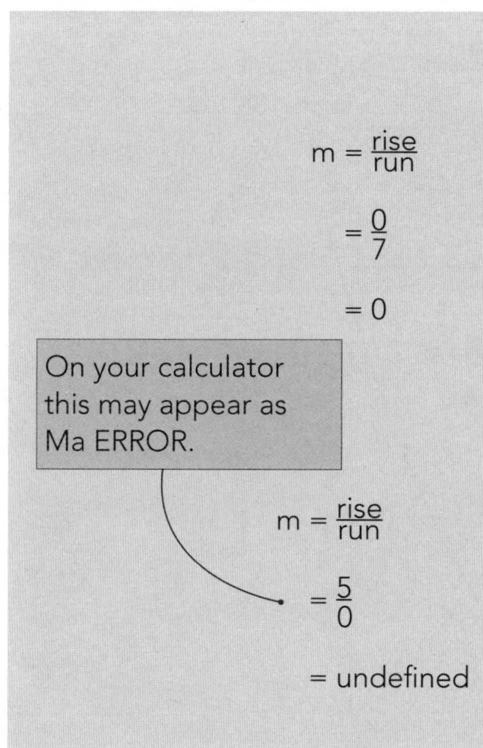

Horizontal lines

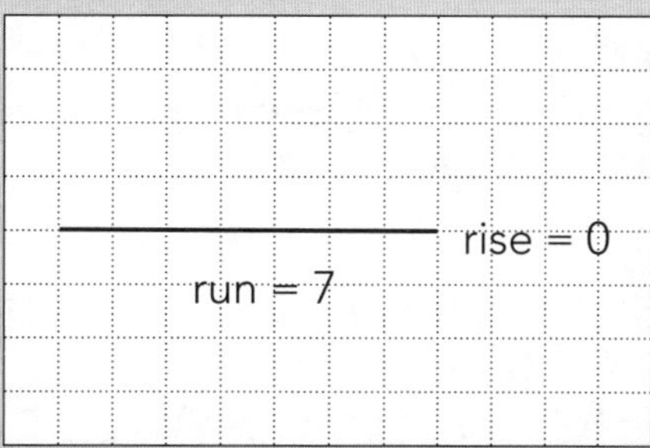

Vertical lines

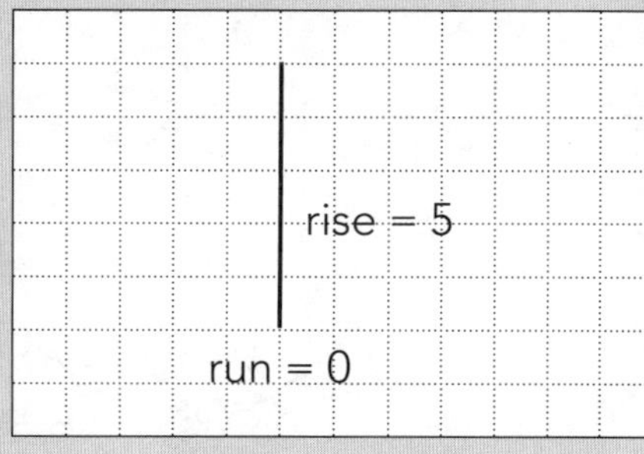

Calculate the gradients of these lines.

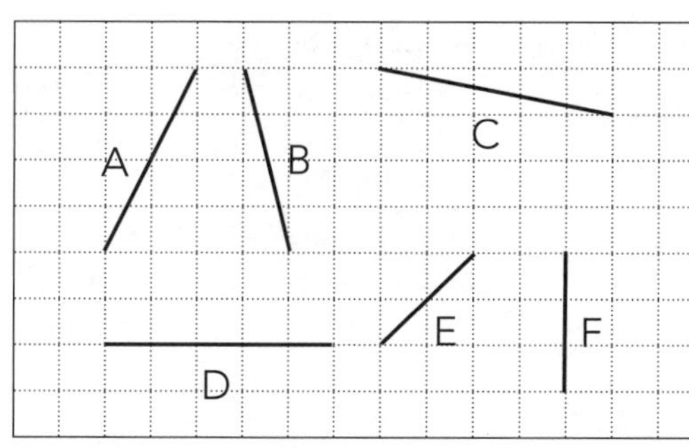

Gradient A = ______________________

Gradient B = ______________________

Gradient C = ______________________

Gradient D = ______________________

Gradient E = ______________________

Gradient F = ______________________

Draw line segments to show these gradients.

A $m = \frac{1}{2}$

B $m = -2$

C $m = \frac{2}{5}$

D $m = -\frac{3}{2}$

E $m = \frac{3}{7}$

F $m = -\frac{5}{9}$

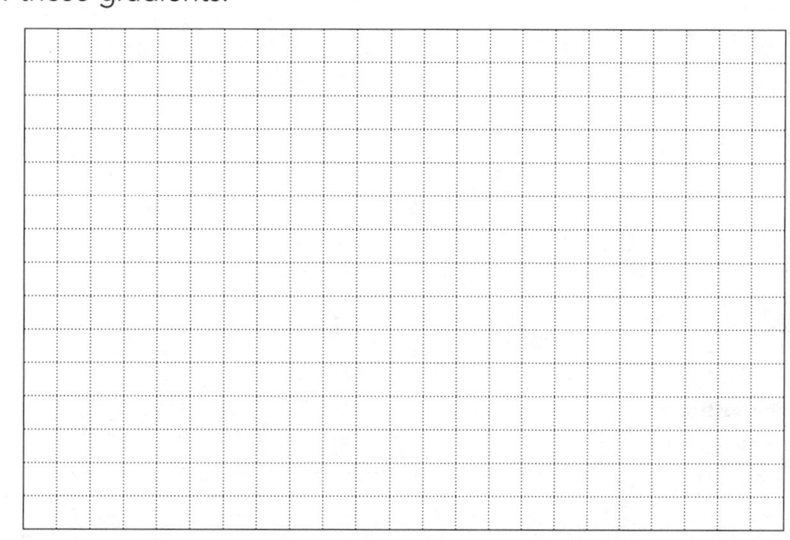

Gradient function of a parabola

Use the tangents drawn at each point to check the gradients given in the table below.

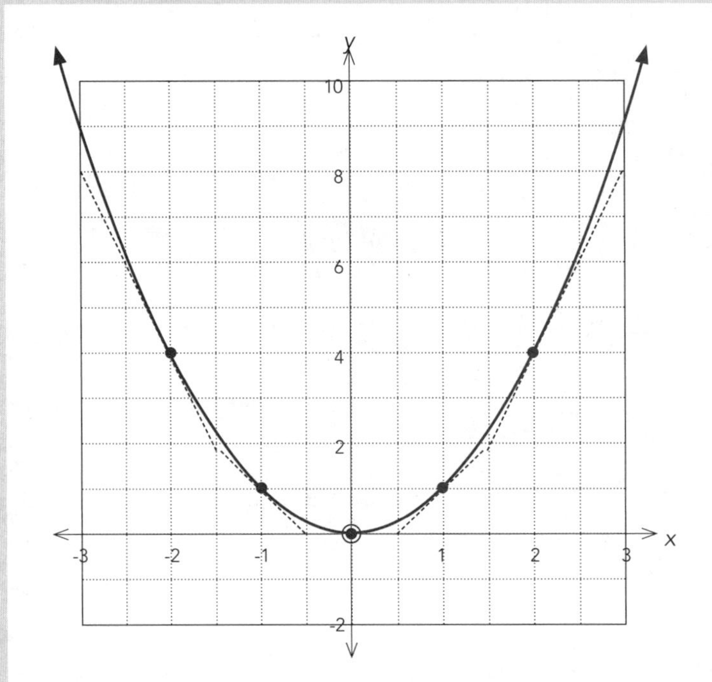

x value	-2	-1	0	1	2	x
y value	4	1	0	1	4	x^2
Gradient	-4	-2	0	2	4	2x

Rule

Graph of the gradients:

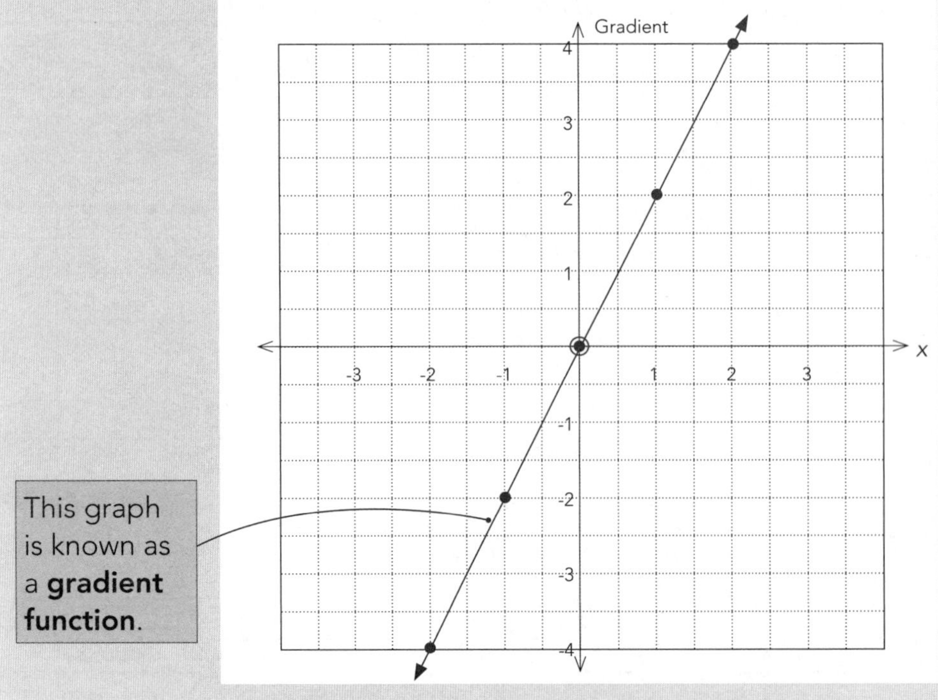

 ISBN: 9780170354233

Sketching gradient functions of curves

To find the gradient function of a graph:

1. Sketch tangents at a range of points on the graph, particularly where there is a turning point.
2. Write beside each point whether the gradient is positive, negative or zero.
3. Transfer these onto the gradient function graph.

Example one: A quadratic

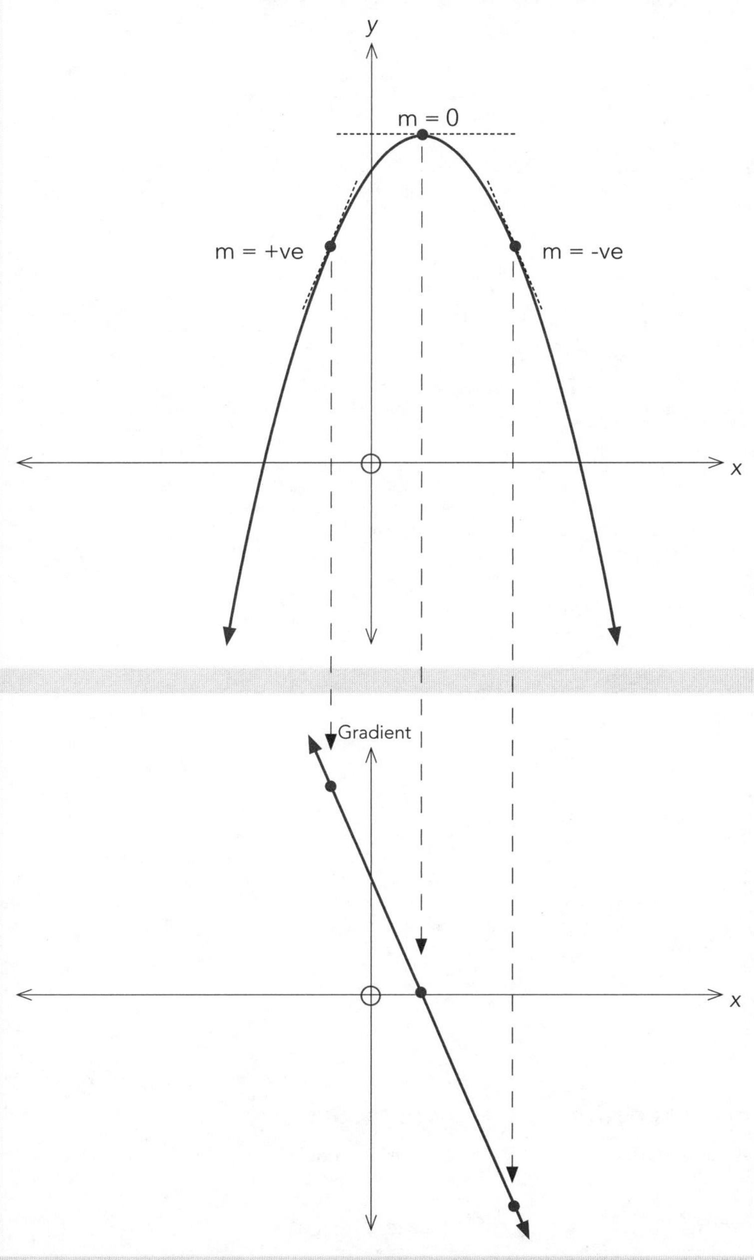

'Sketch the gradient function' for a parabola means:

1. You must get the x-intercept correct. This will correspond with the maximum or minimum.
2. You must have a straight line if the original is a parabola.
3. The gradient must have the correct sign, but its size (the slope) does not matter unless you are given the equation of the original function.

ISBN: 9780170354233

Example two: A cubic

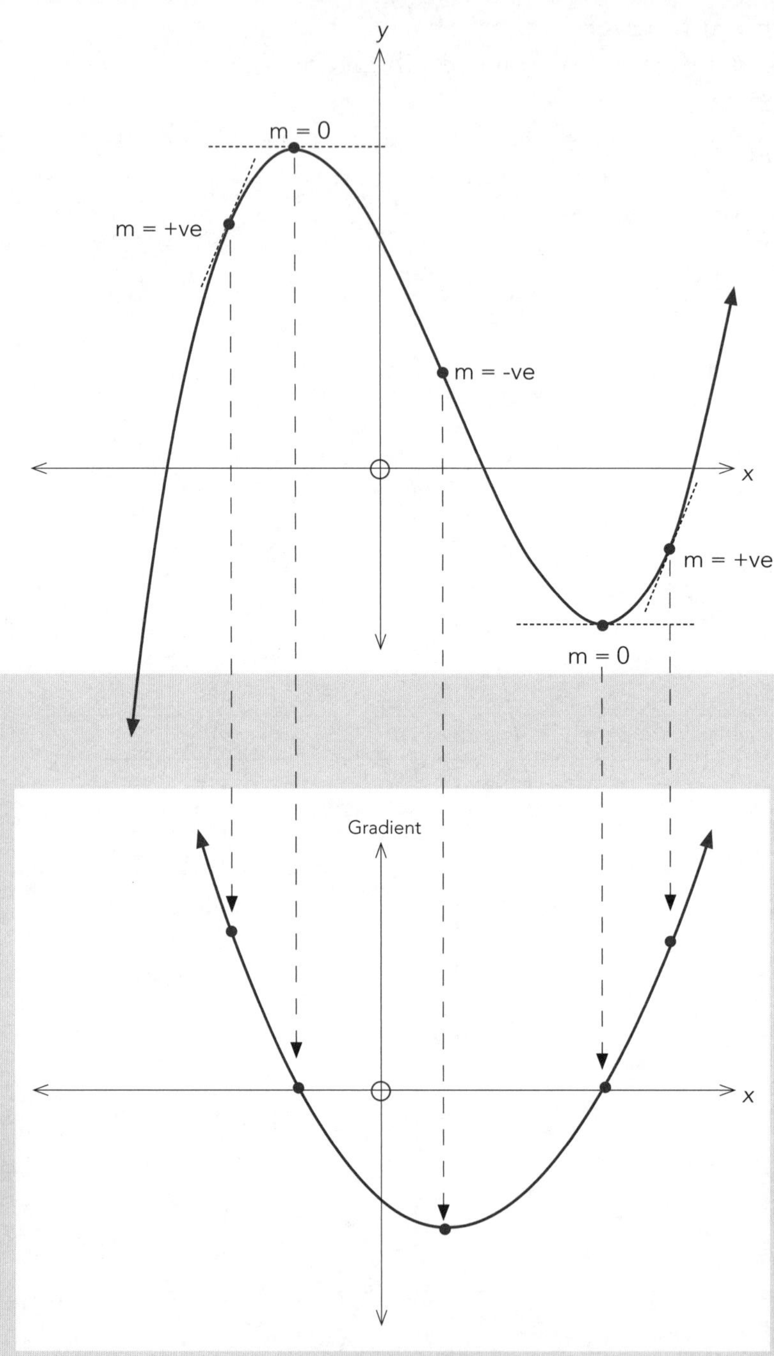

'Sketch the gradient function' for a cubic means:

1. You must get the x-intercepts correct. These will correspond with the maximum or minimum.
2. You must have a parabola if the original is a cubic.
3. The parabola must be the correct way up.

ISBN: 9780170354233

Sketch gradient functions for the following.

1

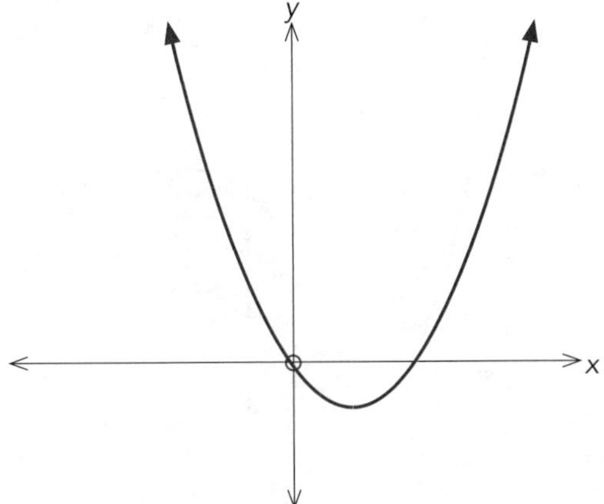

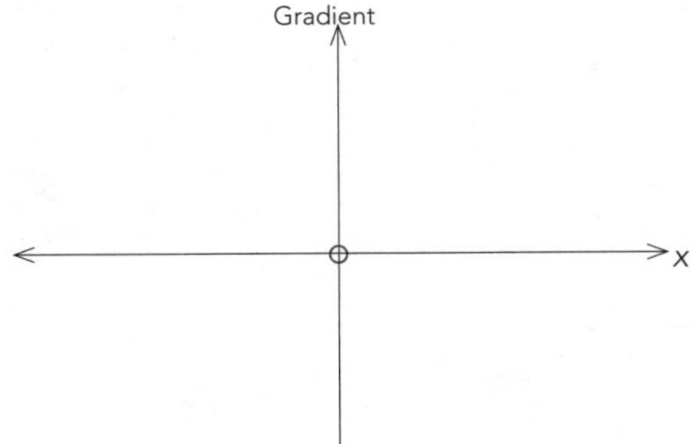

2

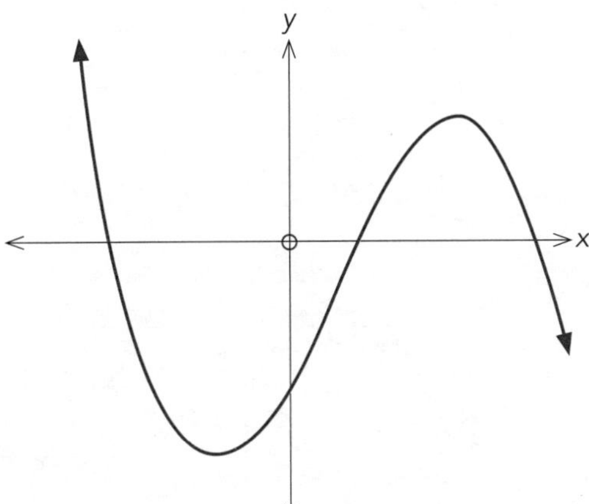

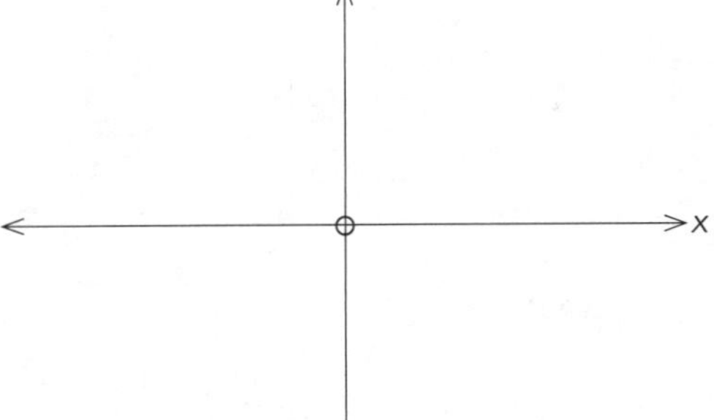

3

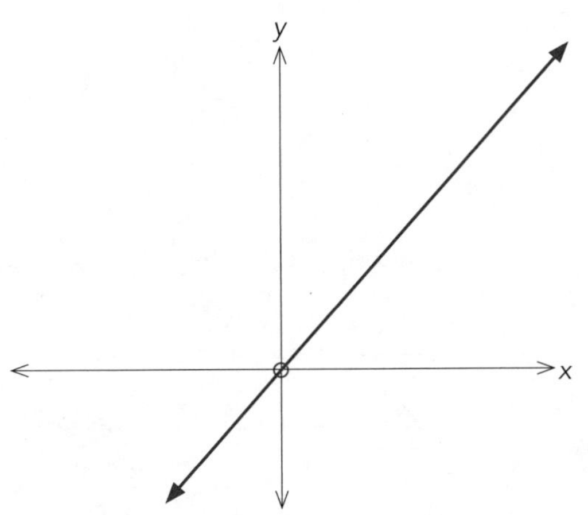

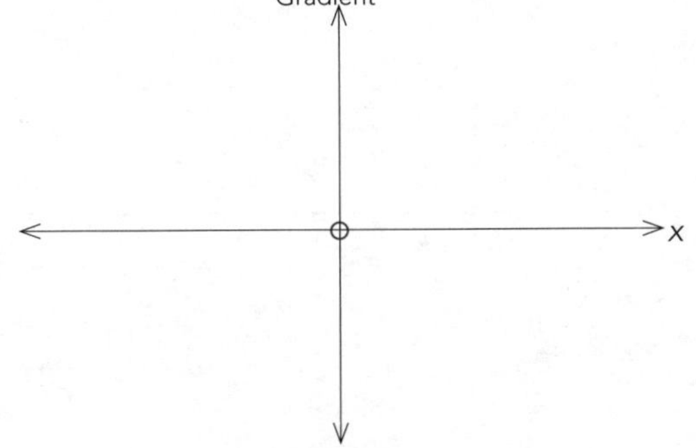

4

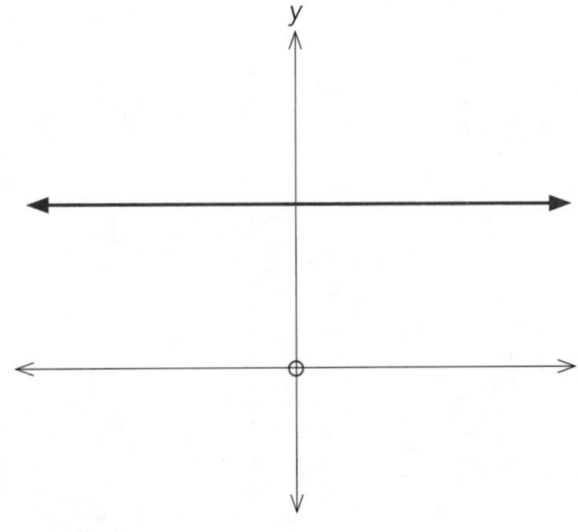

Gradient

x

ISBN: 9780170354233

5

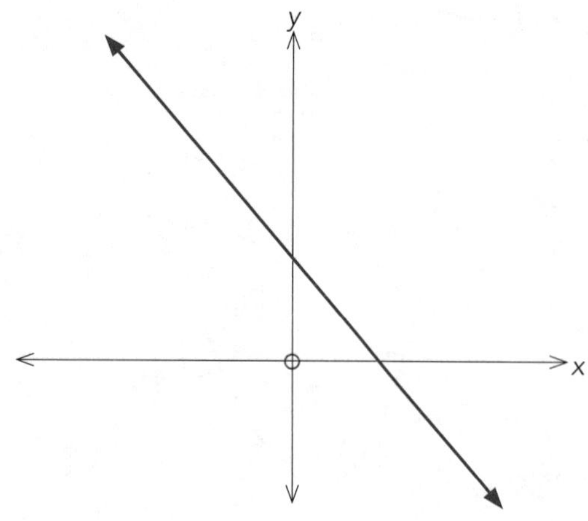

6

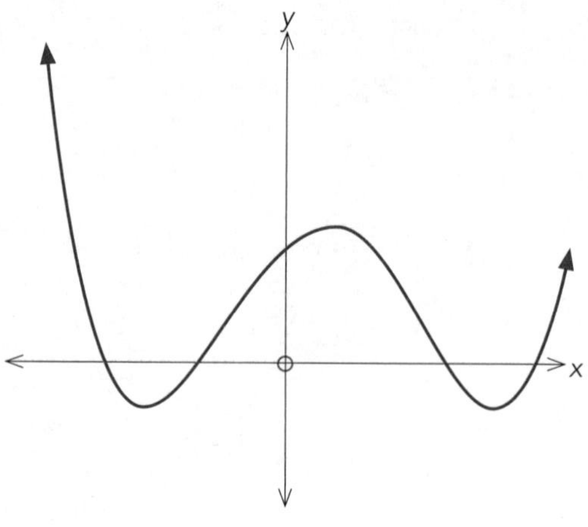

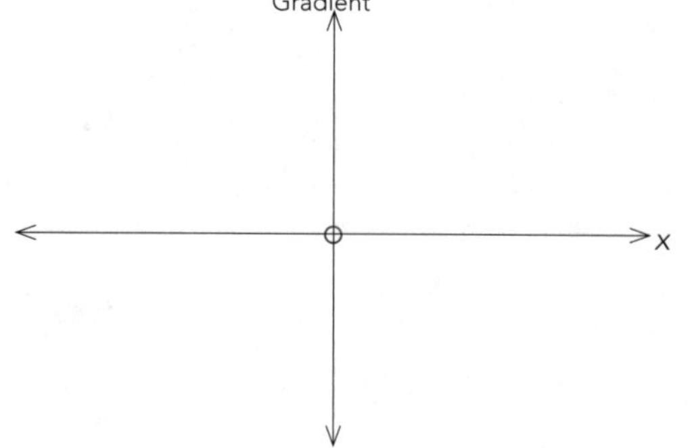

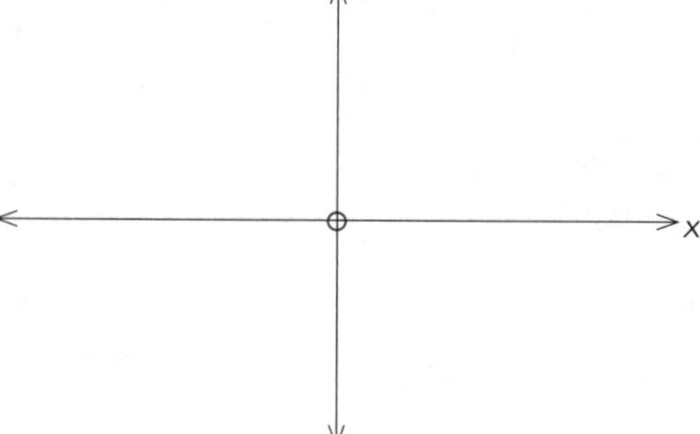

7

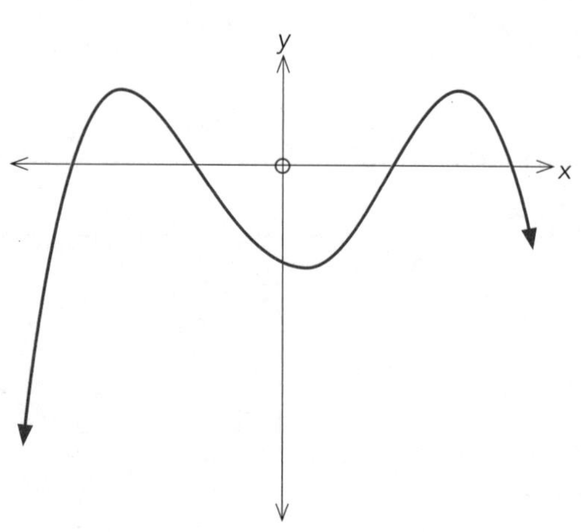

8

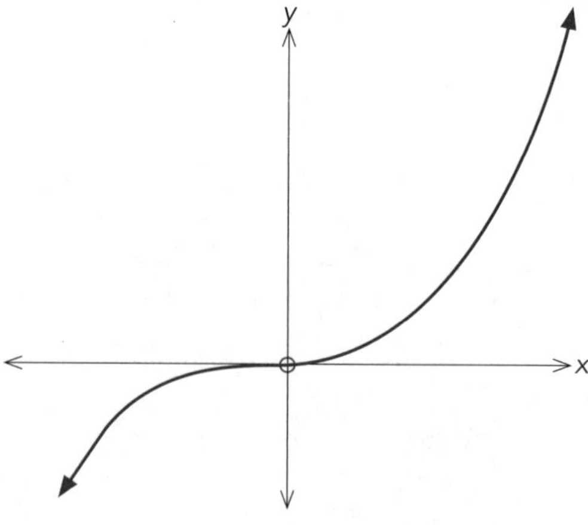

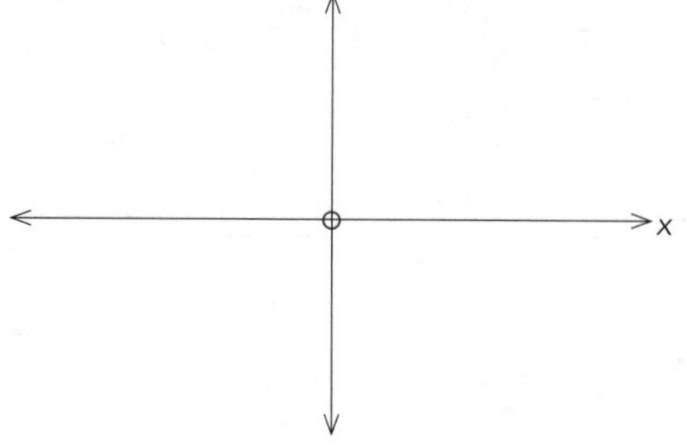

Gradient

x

ISBN: 9780170354233

Calculus — the mathematics of change

The gradient function shows how one parameter is changing with respect to another. For example:

1 The height of a plane during a steady climb as time changes.

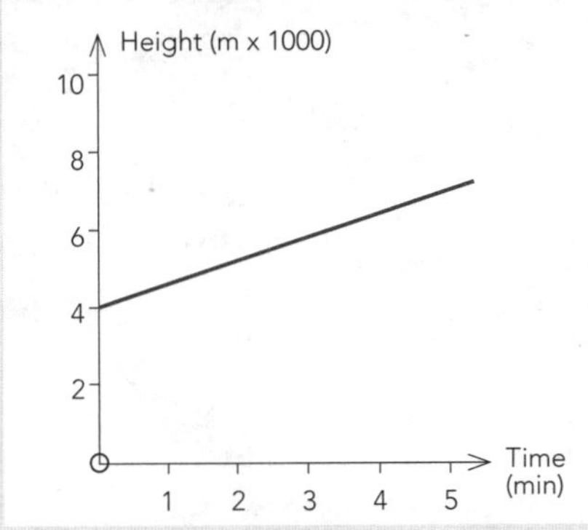

The **change** in height is 600 m/min.

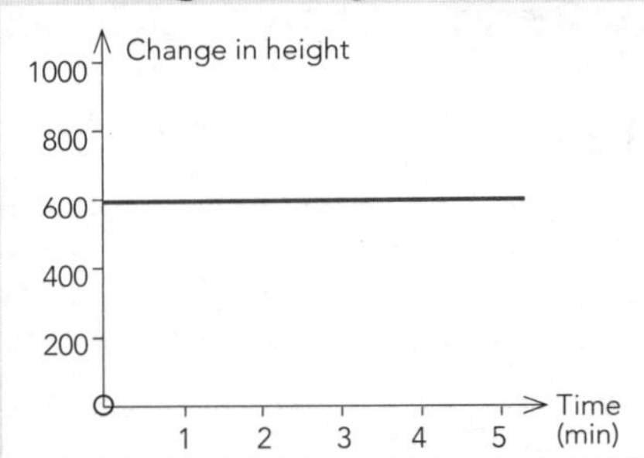

2 The trajectory of a ball thrown up from a balcony until lands on the ground.

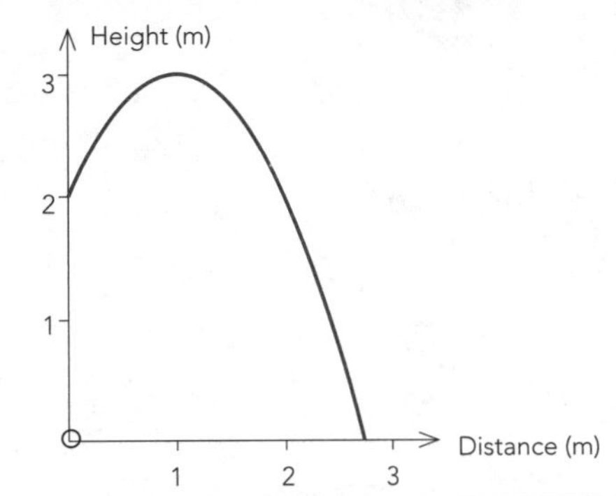

The **change** in height of the ball.

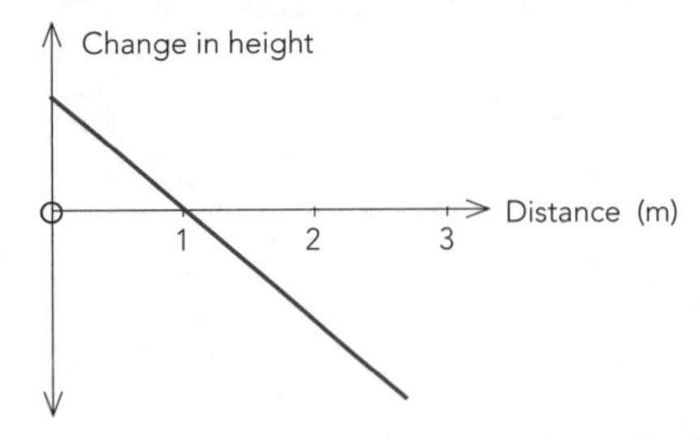

3 The height of a roller coaster above the ground.

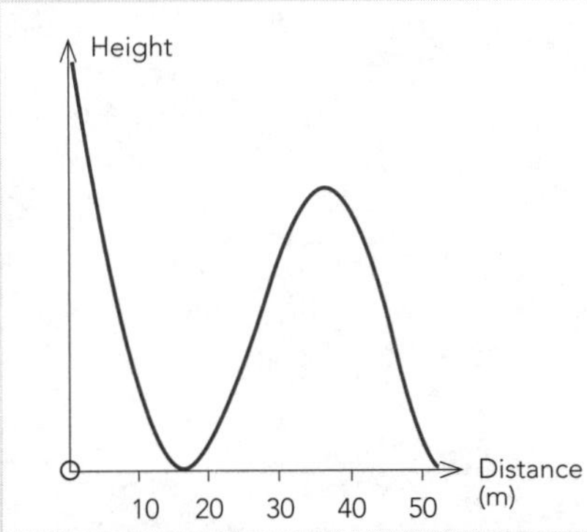

The **change** in height

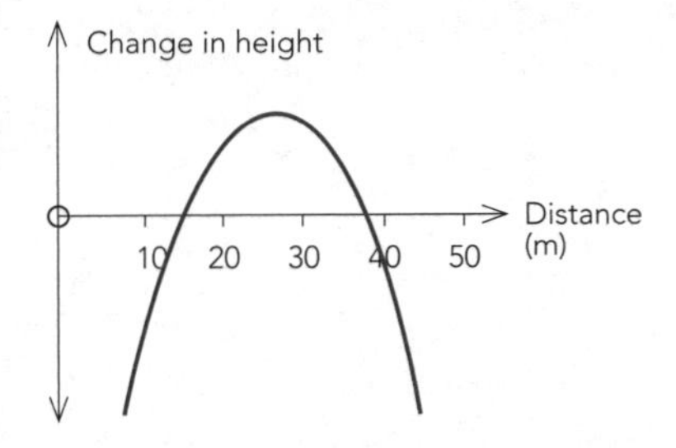

4 The number of bacteria in a test tube.

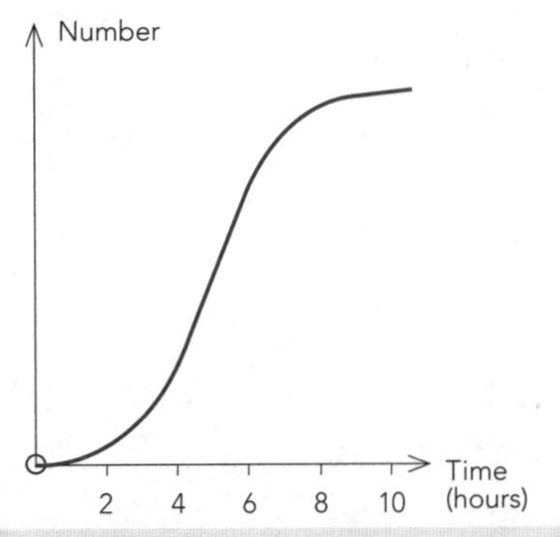

The **rate** of growth of the bacterial population.

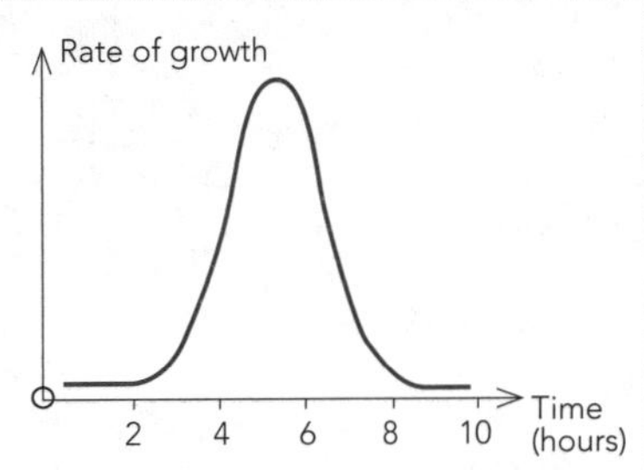

ISBN: 9780170354233

Terminology

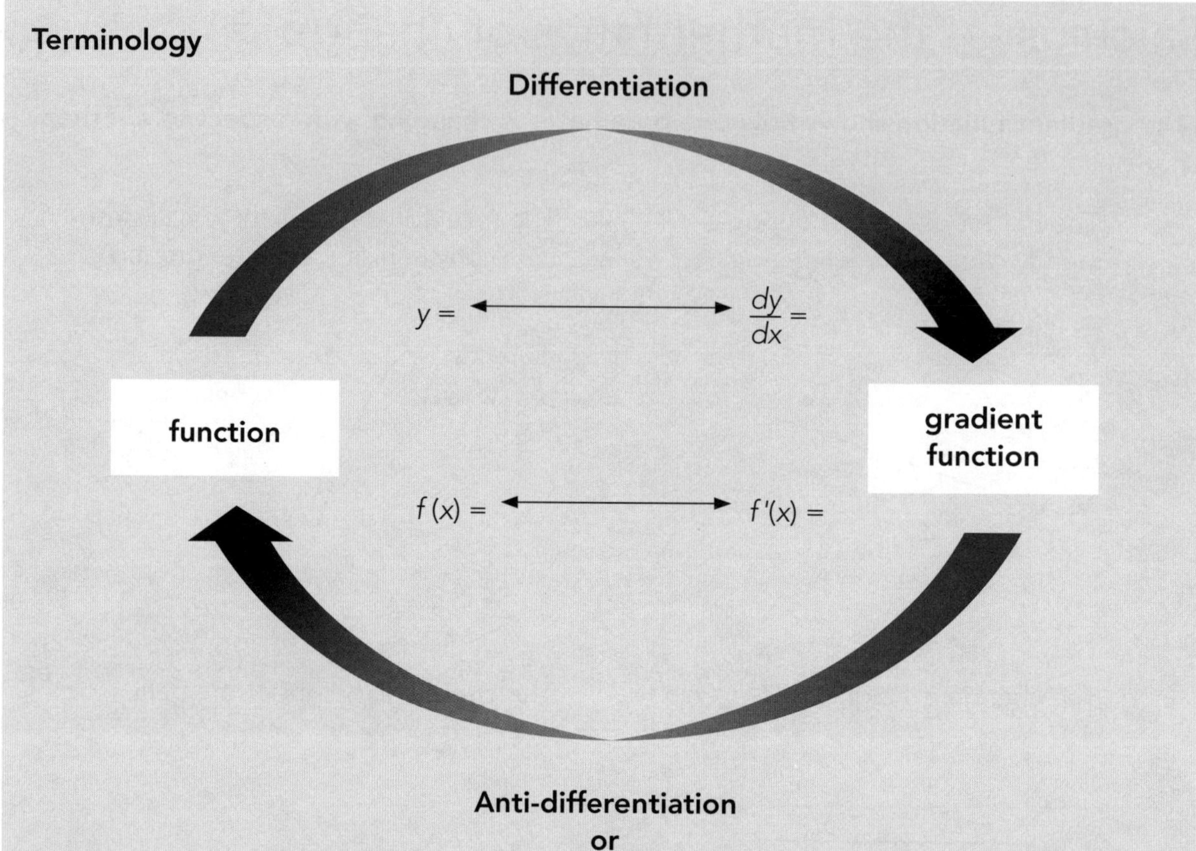

Anti-differentiation or Integration

Conventions:

- If the function is expressed as $y =$…., then the gradient function is expressed as $\frac{dy}{dx} =$ ….

  For example:

$$y = x^2 \longrightarrow \frac{dy}{dx} = 2x$$

- If the function is expressed as $f(x) =$ …., then the gradient function is expressed as $f'(x) =$ ….

  For example:

$$f(x) = x^2 \longrightarrow f'(x) = 2x$$

ISBN: 9780170354233

Differentation

Differentiating a polynomial

The rule:

Let $\mathbf{y = ax^b}$.

1 Multiply the coefficient by the exponent: a x b = ab.
Write this as the new coefficient.
2 Subtract one from the exponent: b – 1.
Write this as the new exponent.
3 If there are several terms, just differentiate each separately.

So $\mathbf{y = ax^b} \longrightarrow \mathbf{\frac{dy}{dx} = abx^{b-1}}$

or $\mathbf{f(x) = ax^b} \longrightarrow \mathbf{f'(x) = abx^{b-1}}$

Some tricks:

1 x^3 means $1x^3$, so $f(x) = x^3 \longrightarrow f'(x) = 3x^2$

2 x means x^1 and $x^0 = 1$, so $f(x) = 7x \longrightarrow f'(x) = 7$

3 Constants, e.g. 4, can be written as $4x^0$, so $f(x) = 4 \longrightarrow f'(x) = 0$

Examples:

1 $y = 5x^3 \longrightarrow \frac{dy}{dx} = 15x^2$

2 $f(x) = 3x^4 \longrightarrow f'(x) = 12x^3$

3 $y = x^5 + 2x \longrightarrow \frac{dy}{dx} = 5x^4 + 2$

4 $f(x) = 9x + 1 \longrightarrow f'(x) = 9$

5 $f(x) = 10 - x \longrightarrow f'(x) = -1$

Differentiate the following polynomials.

1 $y = 7x^3$ ______________________________

2 $f(x) = x^2$ ______________________________

3 $y = 9x^5$ ______________________________

4 $f(x) = 10$ ______________________________

5 $y = 23x$ ______________________________

6 $f(x) = 3x^8 + 5x$ ______________________________

7 $y = 6x^5 + 4x - 2$ ______________________________

8 $f(x) = 7 - 0.15x$ ______________________________

9 $y = -8 - 2x + 11x^2$ ______________________________

Some more tricks:

1 Fractions: $\frac{x^2}{3}$ can be written as $\frac{1}{3}x^2$, so $f(x) = \frac{x^2}{3} \longrightarrow f'(x) = \frac{2}{3}x$

2 Brackets: expand these before differentiating.

$$f(x) = \frac{1}{4}(20 - x) = 5 - \frac{1}{4}x \longrightarrow f'(x) = -\frac{1}{4}$$

Examples:

1 $y = \frac{3x^5}{10} = \frac{3}{10}x^5 \longrightarrow \frac{dy}{dx} = \frac{15}{10}x^4 = \frac{3}{2}x^4$

2 $f(x) = \frac{x^2 + x}{4} = \frac{1}{4}(x^2 + x) = \frac{1}{4}x^2 + \frac{1}{4}x \longrightarrow f'(x) = \frac{1}{2}x + \frac{1}{4}$

3 $y = (2x - 1)(x + 3) = 2x^2 + 5x - 3 \longrightarrow \frac{dy}{dx} = 4x + 5$

4 $f(x) = 0.1x(2 - x^3) = 0.2x - 0.1x^4 \longrightarrow f'(x) = 0.2 - 0.4x^3$

  ISBN: 9780170354233

10 $f(x) = x^3 - 8x^2 + 23x - 4$ ______________________________

11 $y = \frac{x}{2}$ ______________________________

12 $f(x) = \frac{x^4}{5} + 2x$ ______________________________

13 $y = 7 - \frac{9x^3}{10}$ ______________________________

14 $f(x) = \frac{10x^2 + x}{10}$ ______________________________

15 $y = x(2 - 3x)$ ______________________________

16 $f(x) = -3(x^2 + 2x - 1)$ ______________________________

17 $y = \frac{-x^5 + 3}{10}$ ______________________________

18 $f(x) = 0.001(5x^2 + 4x - 3)$ ______________________________

19 $y = 5 - 0.1(x + 4)$ ______________________________

20 $f(x) = \frac{7(x^4 - x)}{10}$ ______________________________

21 $y = 1 + \frac{2x^5 + 10x}{5}$ ______________________________

22 $f(x) = x(x - 4)^2$ ______________________________

23 $y = (2x - 3)(5 - 4x)$ ______________________________

24 $y = (7 - 3x)^2$ ______________________________

ISBN: 9780170354233

Using a differentiated polynomial to calculate the gradient

Remember:
- We can find the equation of the gradient function by differentiating the equation of the original function.
- If we substitute values for x into the gradient function, we can find the size of the gradient at a point.

1 Given the equation and a value for x, calculate the gradient

Example: Calculate the gradient of the curve $f(x) = -x^2 + 4$ where $x = 1$ and where $x = -2$.

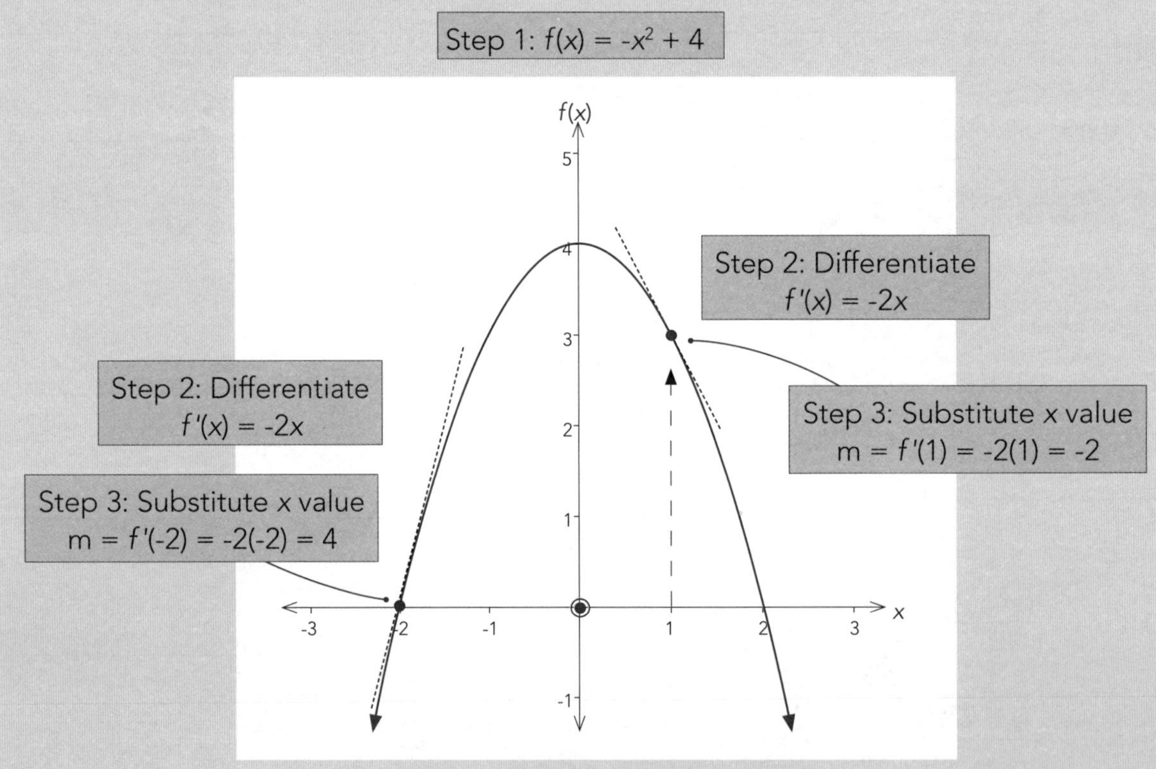

So, where $x = -2$ the gradient is 4, and where $x = 1$ the gradient is -2.

In practice you don't need to draw the graph, although sketching it can be a good check of your answer. Here is an example without drawing the graph.

Calculate the gradient of the tangent to the curve $y = 3x^2 + 4x - 5$:

a where $x = 2$. $\frac{dy}{dx} = 6x + 4 \longrightarrow$ the gradient $= 6(2) + 4 = 16$

b where $x = -1$. $\frac{dy}{dx} = 6x + 4 \longrightarrow$ the gradient $= 6(-1) + 4 = -2$

ISBN: 9780170354233

Calculate the gradient of the following curves at the given values for x.

1 $f(x) = x^3$ where $x = 1$

2 $y = x^2 - 4x + 3$ where $x = -1$

3 $f(x) = 3x^2 - x + 9$ where $x = 0$

4 $y = 8x - 5x^2$ where $x = 2$

5 $f(x) = 12x$ where $x = 5$. Comment on your answer.

6 $y = x(7 - 2x)$ where $x = -2$

7 $f(x) = \frac{x^3 - x}{2}$ where the curve crosses the y-axis

8 $y = (x + 3)(5 - 2x)$ at the point (-1 ,14)

9 $f(x) = \frac{x(x-6)}{3}$ at the point (9 ,9)

10 $y = \frac{1 - x}{4}$ at the point (1, 0)

11 $y = 3x^2 - \frac{x}{4}$ at the point (4 ,47)

12 $f(x) = 1 - x^3$ at the point (2 ,-7)

ISBN: 9780170354233

2 Given the equation and a value for *y*, calculate the gradient

Example: Calculate the gradient of the curve $f(x) = -x^2 + 4$ where $f(x) = 3$.

Step 1: $f(x) = -x^2 + 4$

Step 2: Solve to find x value(s)

$3 = -x^2 + 4$

$x^2 = 1$

$x = \pm 1$

The new bit.

Step 3: Differentiate

$f'(x) = -2x$

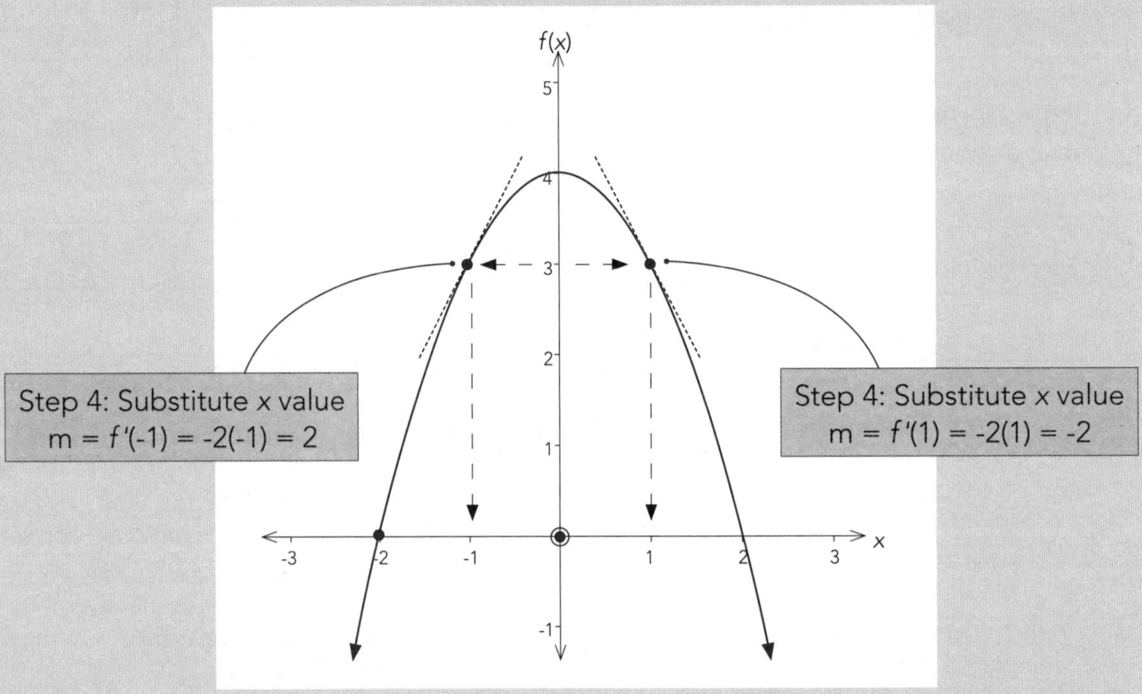

Step 4: Substitute x value

$m = f'(-1) = -2(-1) = 2$

Step 4: Substitute x value

$m = f'(1) = -2(1) = -2$

So, where $f(x) = 3$, the gradient is 2 where $x = -1$, and where $x = 1$ the gradient is -2.

In practice you don't need to draw the graph, although sketching it can be a good check of your answer. Here is an example without drawing the graph.

Calculate the gradient of the tangent to the curve $y = 5x - x^2$ where $y = 0$.

Where $y = 0$: $x(5 - x) = 0$, so $x = 0$ or $x = 5$

$x = 0 \longrightarrow \frac{dy}{dx} = 5 - 2x \longrightarrow$ the gradient $= 5 - 2(0) = 5$

$x = 5 \longrightarrow \frac{dy}{dx} = 5 - 2x \longrightarrow$ the gradient $= 5 - 2(5) = -5$

ISBN: 9780170354233

Calculate the gradient of the following curves at the given values for y.

1 $y = x^2$ where $y = 16$

2 $y = x^3$ where $y = 8$

3 $y = -8x$ where $y = 16$, where $y = 0$, and where $y = -16$. Does this surprise you? Explain your answer.

4 $f(x) = x^2 - 9$ where $f(x) = 0$

5 $y = x(5 - x)$ where the curve crosses the x-axis

6 $f(x) = x^2 + 1$ where $f(x) = 50$

7 $y = (x + 3)(x - 2)$ where $y = 0$

8 $f(x) = (2x - 1)(x + 3)$ where the curve crosses the x-axis

9 $y = 5 - x^2$ where $y = -31$

10 $f(x) = \frac{x^2}{2}$ where $f(x) = 8$

3 Given the equation and coordinates of a point, find the equation of a tangent

Remember, the gradient of a curve at a given point is the same as the gradient of the **tangent** to the curve at that point.

So, if you have the coordinates of a point (x_1, y_1) and the gradient of the tangent at that point (m), you can calculate the equation of the tangent using the formula:

$$\mathbf{y - y_1 = m(x - x_1)}$$

Example one: Find the equation of the tangent to the curve $y = 3x^2 - 2x + 4$ at the point (1, 5).

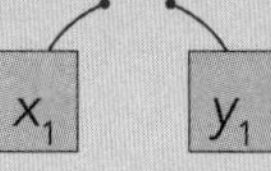

Step 1: Differentiate: $\frac{dy}{dx} = 6x - 2$

Step 2: Find the gradient where $x = 1$: $\frac{dy}{dx} = 6(1) - 2 = 4$

Step 3: Substitute into $y - y_1 = m(x - x_1)$: $y - 5 = 4(x - 1)$

$y - 5 = 4x - 4$

∴ Equation of tangent is: $y = 4x + 1$

Example two: Find the equation of the tangent to the curve $f(x) = x^3 - 2x$ at the point where $x = 2$.

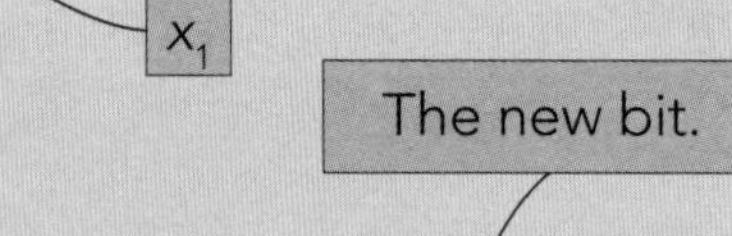

Step 1: Substitute into $f(x)$ to calculate y_1: $y_1 = f(2) = (2)^3 - 2(2) = 4$

∴ Tangent passes through (2, 4)

Step 2: Differentiate: $f'(x) = 3x^2 - 2$

Step 3: Find the gradient where $x = 2$: $f'(x_1) = 3(2)^2 - 2 = 10$

Step 4: Substitute into $y - y_1 = m(x - x_1)$: $y - 4 = 10(x - 2)$

$y - 4 = 10x - 20$

∴ Equation of tangent is: $y = 10x - 16$

ISBN: 9780170354233

Calculate the equation of the tangents to the following curves at the points indicated.

1 $y = x^2$ at the point (3, 9)

2 $f(x) = 2x^3 + 7x$ at the point (1, 9)

3 $y = 5x - x^2$ at the point (-1, -6)

4 $f(x) = 5 - 3x + x^2$ at the point (-1, 9)

5 $y = (x + 3)(x - 2)$ where $x = 3$

6 $g(x) = x^3 - 2x^2 + x$ at the origin

7 $y = 6x^2 - 24$ where $y = 0$

8 $y = -(x + 6)(x - 2)$ where $x = -2$

9 $f(x) = 10 - \frac{x^2}{2}$ at the point (6, -8)

10 $y = -x^3$ where $y = 27$

11 $y = -x\,(x + 3)$ where $x = 1$

12 $y = x\,(x + 1)(x + 2)$ at the point (1, 6)

ISBN: 9780170354233

Using a differentiated polynomial to locate points where the curve has a given gradient

Example one: Find the coordinates of a point on the curve $y = 3x^2 - 2x + 4$ where the gradient is 4.

Step 1: Differentiate: $\frac{dy}{dx} = 6x - 2$

Step 2: $\frac{dy}{dx} = 4$ so substitute and solve:

$$6x - 2 = 4$$
$$6x = 6$$
$$x = 1$$

Step 3: Substitute into $y = 3x^2 - 2x + 4$:

$$y = 3(1)^2 - 2(1) + 4$$
$$y = 5$$

So the gradient to the curve $y = 3x^2 - 2x + 4$ is 4 at the point (1, 5).

Example two: Find the coordinates of the points on the curve $f(x) = x^3 - 8x - 3$ where the gradient is 19.

Step 1: Differentiate: $f'(x) = 3x^2 - 8$

Step 2: $f'(x) = 19$, so substitute and solve:

$$3x^2 - 8 = 19$$
$$3x^2 = 27$$
$$x^2 = 9$$
$$x = \pm 3$$

Step 3: Substitute into $f(x) = x^3 - 8x - 3$:

$$f(x) = (3)^3 - 8(3) - 3$$
$$f(x) = 0$$

or:

$$f(x) = (-3)^3 - 8(-3) - 3$$
$$f(x) = -6$$

So the gradient to the curve $f(x) = x^3 - 8x - 3$ is 19 at the points (-3, -6) and (3, 0).

ISBN: 9780170354233

Locate the points where the curves have the given gradients.

1 $y = x^2$ where m = 6

2 $f(x) = 5x^2 + 2x$ where the gradient is 22

3 $y = 0.5x^2 - 5x + 3$ where the gradient is -3

4 $y = -x^2 + 4x - 7$ where the gradient is horizontal

5 $g(x) = 3x^2 + 5x + 7$ where m = -1

6 $y = 10x - 7x^2$ where the gradient is -4

7 $h(x) = 11 + x - \frac{1}{3}x^3$ where the gradient is 0

8 $y = -2x^3$ where the gradient is -24

9 $f(x) = 10 - \frac{x^3}{2}$ where the gradient is -13.5.

10 $y = 5 - \frac{x^3}{3}$ where the gradient is -16.

11 $y = x(x^2 + 1)$ where m = 4

12 $y = \frac{1}{3}x^3 - x^2$ where m = 0

ISBN: 9780170354233

Putting it all together

1 Find the coordinates of a point on the curve $y = 11 - 3x + 0.5x^2$ where the gradient is -4.

2 Find the equation of the tangent to the curve $f(x) = 3x(x - 4)$ where $x = 2$.

3 Find the coordinates of the points on the graph $y = 4x^3 + 2x + 1$ where the gradient is 14.

4 A function g is given by $g(x) = \frac{5x^2 - 3x}{2}$. Find the gradient of the graph of g at the point where the graph crosses the y-axis.

5 Find the equations of the tangents to the curve $y = 2x^2 - 8$ where it crosses the x-axis.

6 Find the coordinates of the point on the graph $y = -5x^2 - 10x + 1$ where the tangent is horizontal.

ISBN: 9780170354233

7 Find the equation of the tangent to the curve $f(x) = x^3 - 4x^2 + 3x + 1$ at the point (1, 1).

8 Find the equation of the tangent to the curve $y = x^4 - x^2 - 6$ where $x = 1$.

9 Find the coordinates of the points on the graph $y = -x^3 + 15x$ where the gradient is equal to three.

10 A function h is given by $h(x) = \dfrac{4x^2 - 2x - 3}{5}$. Find the gradient of the graph of h at the point where $x = -3$.

11 Find the equation of the tangent to the curve $f(x) = -x^3 + 27$ where $y = 0$.

12 Find the gradient of the graph $y = (x + 1)(x + 2)$ where it crosses the y-axis.

ISBN: 9780170354233

Locating turning points and determining their nature

Increasing and decreasing functions

- A function is increasing where its gradient is positive, and decreasing where its gradient is negative.
- Where it changes from one to the other, we get a turning point.
- Turning points may be maxima or minima.

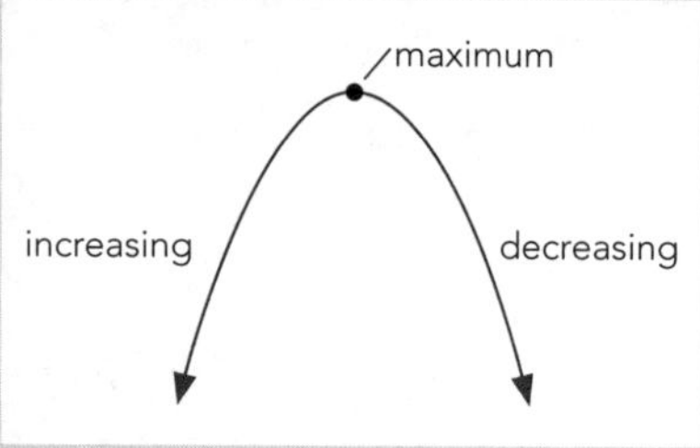

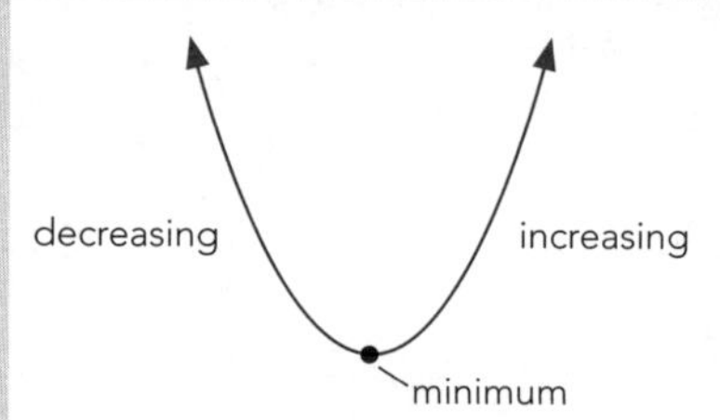

Locate turning points

At turning points the tangent to the curve is horizontal, which means that the gradient = 0.

We can use this to calculate the coordinates of turning points.

Example: Calculate the coordinates of the turning point of the curve $f(x) = 3x^2 + 18x - 1$ and determine its nature.

Step 1: Differentiate: $f'(x) = 6x + 18$

Step 2: Calculate x coordinate: $6x + 18 = 0$

$x = -3$

Step 3: Calculate y coordinate: $f(x) = 3(-3)^2 + 18(-3) - 1$

$f(x) = -28$

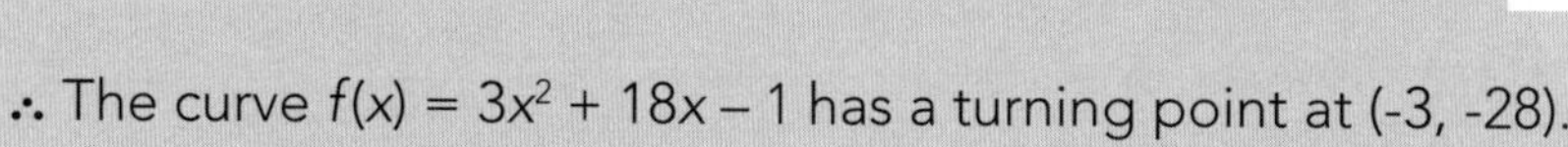

∴ The curve $f(x) = 3x^2 + 18x - 1$ has a turning point at (-3, -28).

Find the nature of a turning point

We can do this by finding the gradient either side of the turning point.

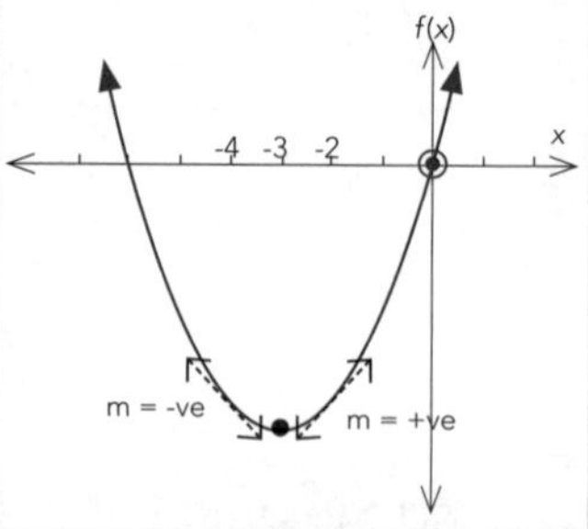

The turning point in the example above is where $x = -3$.
We calculate the gradient where $x = -4$ and where $x = -2$.

Step 1: Calculate gradient to the left:
$x = -4 \longrightarrow f'(x) = 6(-4) + 18 = -6 \longrightarrow$ decreasing function

Step 2: Calculate gradient to the right:
$x = -2 \longrightarrow f'(x) = 6(-2) + 18 = +6 \longrightarrow$ increasing function

With a decreasing function on the left and an increasing function on the right, the turning point *must* be a minimum.

 ISBN: 9780170354233

Example: Calculate the coordinates of the turning points of the curve $y = x^3 - 3x^2 - 9x + 11$ and determine their nature.

Locate the turning point

Step 1: Differentiate: $\frac{dy}{dx} = 3x^2 - 6x - 9$

Step 2: Calculate x coordinate:
$3x^2 - 6x - 9 = 0$
$3(x^2 - 2x - 3) = 0$
$3(x + 1)(x - 3) = 0$
$x = -1$ or $x = 3$

Step 3: Calculate y coordinate:
$y = (-1)^3 - 3(-1)^2 - 9(-1) + 11 = 16$
$y = (3)^3 - 3(3)^2 - 9(3) + 11 = -16$

$\therefore$ The curve $y = x^3 - 3x^2 - 9x + 11$ has turning points at (-1, 16) and (3, -16).

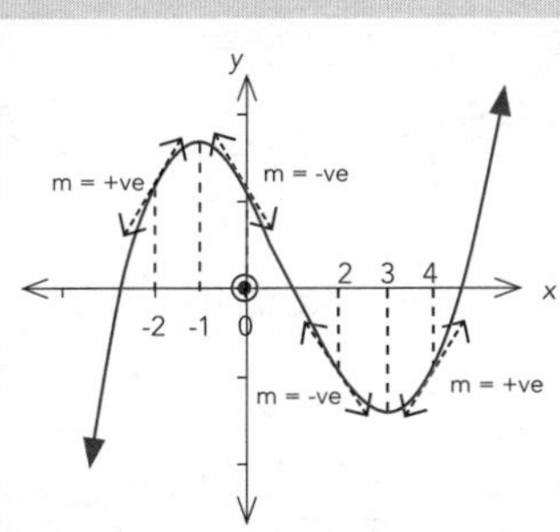

Find the nature of a turning point
The turning points are where $x = -1$ and $x = 3$.

Where $x = -1$:

Step 1: Calculate gradient to the left:
$x = -2 \longrightarrow y = 3(-2)^2 - 6(-2) - 9 = 15 \longrightarrow$ increasing function

Step 2: Calculate gradient to the right:
$x = 0 \longrightarrow y = 3(0)^2 - 6(0) - 9 = -9 \longrightarrow$ decreasing function

With an increasing function on the left and a decreasing function on the right, the turning point at (-1, 16) *must* be a maximum.

Where $x = 3$:

Step 1: Calculate gradient to the left:
$x = 2 \longrightarrow y = 3(2)^2 - 6(2) - 9 = -9 \longrightarrow$ decreasing function

Step 2: Calculate gradient to the right:
$x = 4 \longrightarrow y = 3(4)^2 - 6(4) - 9 = 15 \longrightarrow$ increasing function

With a decreasing function on the left and an increasing function on the right, the turning point at (3, -16) *must* be a minimum.

Your teacher may show you other methods for determining the nature of turning points.

ISBN: 9780170354233

For the following curves, locate the turning points and determine their nature.

1 $y = x^2 - 8x + 3$

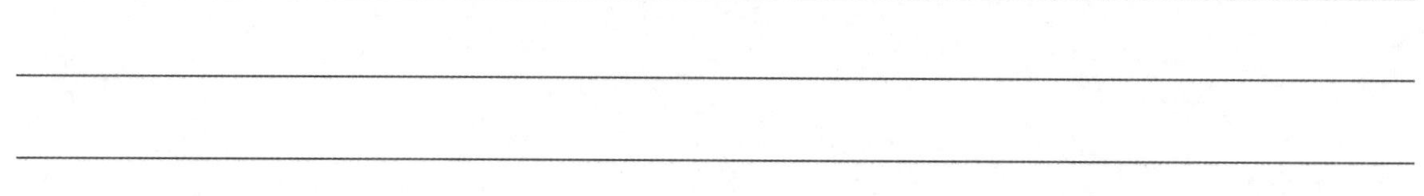

2 $f(x) = 12x + x^2$

3 $y = x^3 - 27x + 10$

4 $g(x) = x^3 + 6x^2 - 15$

5 $y = -x^3 - 6x^2 + 15x - 1$

ISBN: 9780170354233

Finding where functions are increasing or decreasing

What you have learnt in the previous exercise can also be used to determine where functions are increasing.

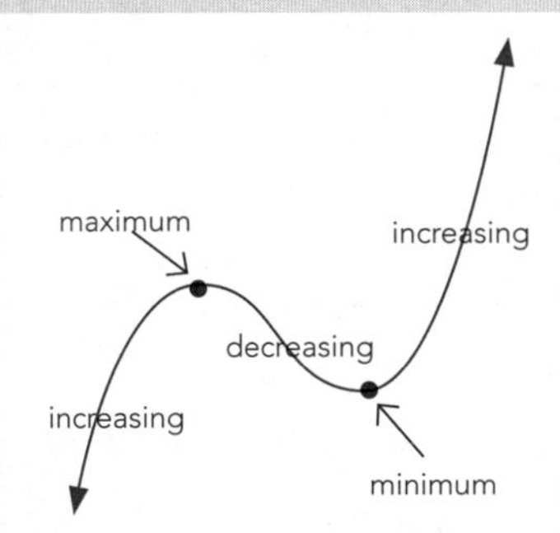

- Remember, the points that separate where a function is increasing from where it is decreasing are the turning points.
- We find the x coordinates of the turning points and then the gradient between them.
- There is no need to find the y coordinates of the turning points, nor their nature unless you are asked for them.

Example: Determine the values for which the function $f(x) = x^3 - 4.5x^2 - 12x + 8$ is decreasing.

Step 1: Differentiate: $f'(x) = 3x^2 - 9x - 12$

Step 2: Calculate x coordinate:

$3x^2 - 9x - 12 = 0$
$3(x^2 - 3x - 4) = 0$
$3(x + 1)(x - 4) = 0$
$x = -1$ or $x = 4$

Step 3: Calculate gradients:

To the left of $x = -1$ Let $x = -2$
$\rightarrow f'(-2) = 3(-2)^2 - 9(-2) - 12 = 18 \rightarrow$ increasing

Between $x = -1$ and $x = 4$ Let $x = 0$
$\rightarrow f'(0) = 3(0)^2 - 9(0) - 12 = -12 \rightarrow$ decreasing

To the right of $x = 4$ Let $x = 5$
$\rightarrow f'(5) = 3(5)^2 - 9(5) - 12 = 18 \rightarrow$ increasing

$\therefore$ The function $f(x) = x^3 - 4.5x^2 - 12x + 8$ is decreasing where $-1 < x < 4$.

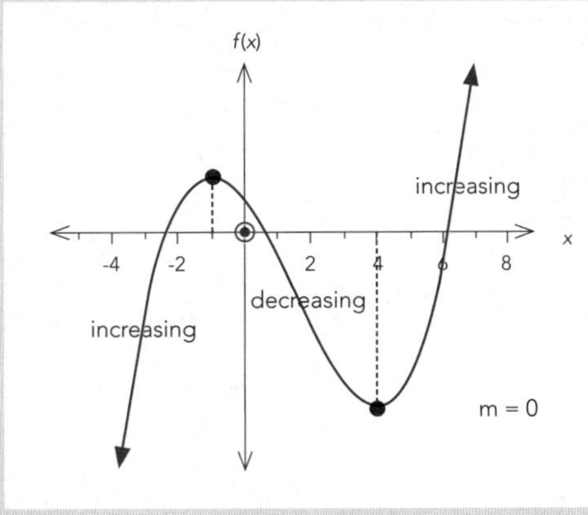

ISBN: 9780170354233

For what values of x are the following functions increasing/decreasing?

1 Decreasing: $y = -x^2 + 8x + 3$

2 Increasing: $f(x) = 12x - x^2$

3 Increasing: $y = x^3 - 3x + 10$

4 Decreasing: $g(x) = x^3 + 6x^2 - 15$

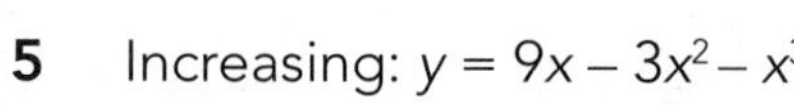

5 Increasing: $y = 9x - 3x^2 - x^3$

ISBN: 9780170354233

Applications

1 Rates of change

- The gradient of a function ($\frac{dy}{dx}$ or $f'(x)$) tells us how fast the variable on the y-axis is changing compared with that on the x-axis.
- You may be told the value of x.
- Alternatively, you may have to calculate the value of x from either the value of y or the value of $\frac{dy}{dx}$.
- A positive value for $\frac{dy}{dx}$ ⟶ the rate is **increasing**.
- A negative value for $\frac{dy}{dx}$ ⟶ the rate is **decreasing**.

Example: If $y = x^2 - 4x - 1$,

$$\frac{dy}{dx} = 2x - 4.$$

Where $x = 3$,

$$\frac{dy}{dx} = 2(3) - 4 = 2.$$

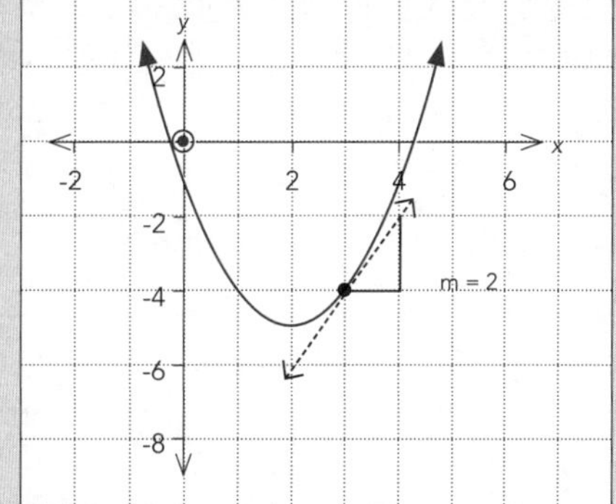

This means that at the point (3, -4), if x increases by 1 unit, then y increases by 2 units.

Using differentiation we can discover the rate of change at any point along a curve.

Note: We do not have to use x and y as our variables. They can take any letters.

There are three types of problems:

a: Where we are given the value of x (or in this case, L)

Example: The surface area of a cube changes as the length of the side increases:

$$A = 6L^2$$

Find the rate of change in the surface area with respect to the length of the side when the **side is 5 cm**.

Given L

Step 1: Differentiate the function: $\frac{dA}{dL} = 12L$

Step 2: Substitute $L = 5$ into the derived function: $\frac{dA}{dL} = 12(5) = 60$

∴ When the side of the cube is 5 cm, the surface area is increasing at 60 cm^2 per cm.

ISBN: 9780170354233

Try these questions.

1 The volume of a cube (V) depends on the length of each side (x). Calculate the rate of change in the volume when each side of the cube is 5 cm.

2 A stone is thrown from the top of a 100 m cliff into the sea. Its height is given by the function $H = 100 - 10t^2$, where t is time in seconds since the stone was thrown. Calculate the rate at which its height is changing after 1.5 seconds.

3 An object falls into a lake. Circular ripples spread out over the lake from the point of impact. The area inside the circular ripple is given by the formula $A = \pi r^2$, where the radius is in metres. How fast is the area growing when the radius is 1.5 m? (You may leave π in your answer.)

4 A slow-growing population (P) of animals increases with time (years). The size of the population is given by $P(t) = 100 + 0.6t^2 - 0.004t^3$. How fast is the population changing after 10 years?

 ISBN: 9780170354233

b: Where we are given the value of y (or in this case, $H(t)$)

Example: An object is dropped from a height of 200 m above the ground. Its height (m) above the ground after t seconds is given by:

$$H(t) = 200 - 10t^2$$

Find the rate of change in the height with respect to time when the object is **110 m above the ground**.

Given H

Step 1: Calculate t when $H(t) = 110$ m:

An extra step

$110 = 200 - 10t^2$
$10t^2 = 90$
$t = 3$ seconds

Step 2: Differentiate the function: $H'(t) = -20t$

Step 3: Substitute $t = 3$ into the derived function: $H'(t) = -20(3) = -60$ m/s

∴ At a height of 110 m and after 3 seconds, the object's height is decreasing at 60 m per second.

Try these questions.

1 The volume of a cube (V) depends on the length of each side (x). Calculate the rate at which the volume is changing when the volume is 512 cm^3.

2 A stone is thrown from the top of a 100 m cliff into the sea. Its height is given by the function $H = 110 - 10t^2$, where t is seconds since the stone was thrown. Calculate the rate at which its height is changing when the stone is 30 m above sea level.

ISBN: 9780170354233

c: Where we are given the value of $\frac{dy}{dx}$ (or in this case, $\frac{dH}{dt}$)

Example: A vase is left under a dripping tap. The height of water in the vase (cm) after t hours is given by the equation:

$$H = 0.2t^2 + 0.5t$$

Find when **the rate of change in the height with respect to time is 2.1 cm per hour**.

Given rate of change ($\frac{dH}{dt}$)

Step 1: Differentiate the function: $\frac{dH}{dt} = 0.4t + 0.5$

Step 2: Solve this when $\frac{dH}{dt}$ = 2.1 cm per hour:

$$0.4t + 0.5 = 2.1$$
$$0.4t = 2.1 - 0.5$$
$$t = 4$$

∴ The height of the water is increasing at 2.1 cm per hour after 4 hours.

Try these questions.

1 The volume of a cube (V) depends on the length of each side (x). Calculate the length of each side when the volume is increasing by 48 cm^3 per cm of side.

2 A stone is thrown from the top of a 100 m cliff into the sea. Its height is given by the function $H = 110 - 5t^2$, where t is seconds since the stone was thrown. Calculate when the stone was dropping at 20 m/s. (Hint: 'dropping' → the rate is negative.)

ISBN: 9780170354233

Mixing it up

1 A patient with a dangerously high temperature of 41°C is given a drug which will reduce his temperature over a period of hours. The relationship between his temperature (T) and the time (h) since he started taking the drug is given by $T = 41 - 0.05h - 0.03h^2$. Calculate the rate at which his temperature is changing five hours after he began taking the drug.

2 A fishpond is being filled by a pipe in its base. The volume (V) of water in it depends on how many minutes (t) the valve in the pipe has been left open. The relationship between these is given by the formula $V = 2t^2 - 0.5t + 11$, where the volume is measured in litres. Calculate the volume of water in the pond when water is entering it at a rate of 11.5 litres/minute.

3 The height of a cylinder is the same as its radius. Its volume can be found by the formula $V = \pi r^3$. Calculate the rate at which the volume is changing when its volume is 125π.

4 The volume of a sphere is given by the formula $V = \frac{4}{3}\pi r^3$. Calculate the radius of the sphere when its volume is increasing by 144π cm^3 per cm of radius.

ISBN: 9780170354233

5 A school canteen buys a supply of 200 juice ice blocks. They become increasingly popular with the students and staff during a hot spell of weather. The remaining stock is given by $N = 200 - 8t - 2t^2$, where t represents time in days and N represents the number of ice blocks remaining. How many ice blocks is the canteen selling per day on day four?

6 The area of a square (cm^2) is given by the formula $A = L^2$, where L is the length of its side. Calculate the length of its side when the area is increasing at 20 cm^2 per cm in length.

7 Miriama is opening a cake stall in the local market. The first week she bakes 15 cakes. The number of cakes she sells each week increases according to the function $N = 15 + 0.01w^3$, where N represents the number of cakes she sells and w is the number of weeks since she started selling them. Calculate the rate of increase in her cake sales when she sells 25 cakes per week.

8 A small business has found that the relationship between the number of items it sells and the amount it spends on advertising (in \$000s) is given by $S(a) = -1.5a^2 + 51a + 100$ when $0 < a < 15$, and a stands for the amount it spends on advertising. How many items can it expect to sell per \$1000 spent on advertising if it spends \$10,000 on advertising?

ISBN: 9780170354233

2 Optimisation

- Optimisation is where we find the highest or lowest value for a function.
- If we plot the function, the highest point will occur at the maximum point on the curve and the lowest point will occur at minimum point.
- We know that at maximum and minimum points, the gradient = 0.

So, we can find where functions are optimised by:

Step 1: Differentiating the function.

Step 2: Calculating the x coordinate by making $\frac{dy}{dx} = 0$.

Step 3: Calculating the y coordinate by substituting into the original function.

You have done all this before, but now you need to use it in a practical situation where the variables are not always x and y.

Example one: A skyrocket is fired from the ground. Its height (in metres) above the ground is given by the relationship $H = 70t - 10t^2$, where t is the time in seconds since it took off. How long did it take to reach its maximum height? Calculate the maximum height reached by the skyrocket.

Step 1: Differentiate: $\frac{dH}{dt} = 70 - 20t$

Step 2: Calculate the x coordinate:

$$70 - 20t = 0$$
$$20t = 70$$
$$t = 3.5 \text{ s}$$

Step 3: Calculate the y coordinate:

$$H = 70(3.5) - 10(3.5)^2$$
$$= 122.5 \text{ m}$$

∴ The rocket took 3.5 seconds to reach a maximum height of 122.5 metres.

Example two: The profit made by a company is estimated to follow the relationship $P(t) = 300 + 12t^2 - t^3$, where P stands for profit (in $000s) and t represents time in years. When is the company expected to make a maximum profit, and how much will this be?

Step 1: Differentiate: $P'(t) = 24t - 3t^2$

Step 2: Calculate the x coordinate:

$$24t - 3t^2 = 0$$
$$t(24 - 3t) = 0$$
$$t = 0 \text{ or } t = 8$$

Step 3: Calculate the y coordinate:

$$t = 0 \rightarrow P(0) = 300$$
$$t = 8 \rightarrow P(8) = 556$$

∴ The maximum profit occurs after 8 years and is $556,000.

Solve these problems.

1 A tunnel needs to be built as part of a cycleway. Its shape is given by the relationship $H = 2.5x(2 - x)$, where H represents height (in metres) and x represents distance from the left side (in metres). Calculate its width and its maximum height.

2 Hannah throws a stone into a lake. The relationship between the distance thrown and the height of the stone (both in metres) is given by the relationship $H = 1 + 0.5x - 0.01x^2$. Calculate the maximum height reached by the stone.

3 The small business in a previous exercise found that the relationship between the number of items it sells and the amount it spends on advertising (in $000s) is given by $S(a) = -1.5a^2 + 51a + 100$. Calculate how much it will need to spend on advertising in order to maximise its sales, and the maximum number of items it can expect to sell.

4 A fish pond is to be constructed in a garden. The relationship between its depth and distance from the edge is given by $D = -1.2x + 0.2x^2$, where D represents depth in metres and x represents distance from the edge. Calculate its maximum depth.

  ISBN: 9780170354233

5 The number of press-ups Adam does per minute in his fitness programme depends on how long he has been doing them. This relationship is given by $N = -0.4t^2 + 2.4t + 10$, where N represents the number of press-ups per minute and t represents time in minutes. How long after he starts is he doing his maximum number of press-ups per minute?

6 Tane is growing a culture of bacteria. He finds that the density of the bacteria in the medium is related to the amount of nutrient added. The relationship is given by the equation $N = 125x - \frac{1}{5}x^3$, where N represents the number of bacteria per millilitre and x is the weight of nutrient in milligrams. Calculate the maximum density of bacteria and the weight of nutrient which is needed to achieve this.

7 A pregnant rabbit manages to swim to a small island. As a result, the population of rabbits on the island is modelled by the relationship $P = 1 + 1.2t^2 - 0.04t^3$, where P represents the number of rabbits and t represents time in years. When will the population peak and what will the maximum number of rabbits be?

8 The volume of a box is proportional to its height. This relationship is given by the equation $V = h^3 - 24h^2 + 144h$, where V represents the volume in cubic centimetres and h represents the height in centimetres. Calculate the maximum and minimum volumes of the box, and the heights at which these occur.

ISBN: 9780170354233

3 Optimisation with related variables

Sometimes you will not be told the equation, but you will need to work it out from the information given to you. The process is best explained by using examples.

Example one: Sam needs to construct a rectangular pen for his two pigs. He has 48 m of fencing available, but he wants his pen to have the **largest area** possible. Calculate the optimum dimensions for his pen.

Area needs to be optimised

Step 1: **Draw a diagram:**

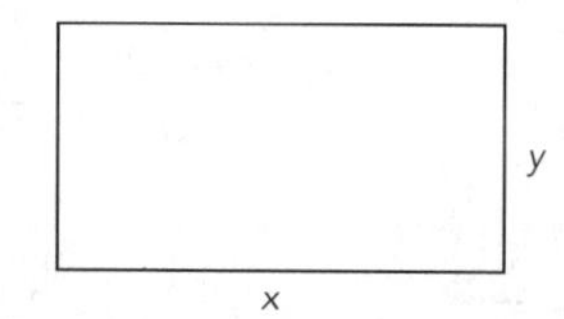

Step 2: **Identify what needs to be optimised, and write an equation for this:**

Area = xy

Problem: This contains two variables, so it cannot be differentiated.

Step 3: **Write an equation which relates x with y:**

$2x + 2y = 48 \rightarrow y = 24 - x$

Step 4: **Substitute for y:**

Area = $x(24 - x)$
$A = 24x - x^2$

So now you have the equation.

Step 5: **Differentiate and calculate maximum and/or minimum:**

$\frac{dA}{dx} = 24 - 2x$ and the maximum will occur where $\frac{dA}{dx} = 0$

so $24 - 2x = 0$

$\therefore x = 12$

Step 6: **Substitute for x into the equation from Step 4 to find the maximum/minimum:**

$A = 24(12) - (12)^2 = 144\text{ m}^2$

Step 7: **Calculate y and test your solution to make sure it works — some solutions don't:**

If $x = 12$ m, then y will also be 12 m, so the pen will be a square.

Step 8: **Answer the question:**

The maximum pen area is 144 m^2, by making a square pen with each side 12 m.

ISBN: 9780170354233

Example two: An airline restricts the size of carry-on baggage by stating that the sum of the dimensions (length + width + depth) must be less than 120 cm. If the base of a carry-on is square, calculate the **maximum volume** possible and the dimensions of this piece of baggage.

Step 1: **Draw a diagram:**

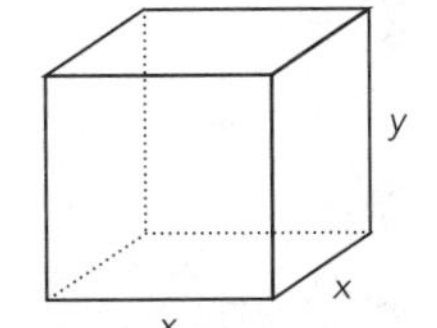

Step 2: **Identify what needs to be optimised, and write an equation for this:**

Volume = x^2y

Step 3: **Write an equation which relates x with *y*:**

$2x + y = 120 \rightarrow y = 120 - 2x$

Step 4: **Substitute for *y*:**

Volume = $x^2(120 - 2x)$

$V = 120x^2 - 2x^3$

Step 5: **Differentiate and calculate maximum and/or minimum:**

$\frac{dV}{dx} = 240x - 6x^2$ and maximum/minimum will occur where $\frac{dV}{dx} = 0$

so $240x - 6x^2 = 0$

$6x(40 - x) = 0$

$\therefore$ either $x = 0$

or $x = 40$

Step 6: **Substitute for x into the equation from Step 4 to find the maximum/mimimum:**

Either $x = 0 \rightarrow V = 120(0)^2 - 2(0)^3 = 0$ m^3

or $x = 40 \rightarrow V = 120(40)^2 - 2(40)^3 = 64{,}000$ cm^3

Step 7: **Calculate *y* and test your solution to make sure it works — some solutions don't:**

If $x = 0$, then there is no baggage — this gives a minimum volume.
If $x = 40$ cm, then $y = 120 - 2(40) = 40$ cm. This results in a cube with sides of 40 cm.

Step 8: **Answer the question:**

The maximum volume of a carry-on piece of baggage is 64,000 cm^3, which is obtained with a cube with sides of 40 cm.

Try these questions.

1 Sam has realised that he can build a bigger rectangular pig pen if he uses an existing fence as one of the sides. If he uses all of his 48 m of fencing, calculate the maximum area of his new pen, and state its dimensions.

Step 1: Draw a diagram:

Step 2: Identify what needs to be optimised, and write an equation for this:

Step 3: Write an equation which relates *x* with *y*:

Step 4: Substitute for *y*:

Step 5: Differentiate and calculate maximum and/or minimum:

Step 6: Substitute for *x* into the equation from Step 4 to find the maximum/minimum:

Step 7: Calculate *y* and test your solution to make sure it works — some solutions don't:

Step 8: Answer the question:

ISBN: 9780170354233

2 A box is constructed so that its length is twice its width. The sum of its length, width and depth is 140 cm. Calculate the values for its dimensions which result in a maximum surface area. Calculate this maximum surface area.

Step 1: **Draw a diagram:**

Step 2: **Identify what needs to be optimised, and write an equation for this:**

Step 3: **Write an equation which relates *x* with *y*:**

Step 4: **Substitute for *y*:**

Step 5: **Differentiate and calculate maximum and/or minimum:**

Step 6: **Substitute for *x* into the equation from Step 4 to find the maximum/minimum:**

Step 7: **Calculate *y* and test your solution to make sure it works — some solutions don't:**

Step 8: **Answer the question:**

ISBN: 9780170354233

3 Zoe has 76 cm of braid to sew around the edge of a rectangular mat. She would like the area of the mat to be as large as possible. Calculate the dimensions which would result in the largest area, and calculate the area of the mat.

Step 1:

Step 2:

Step 3:

Step 4:

Step 5:

Step 6:

Step 7:

Step 8:

ISBN: 9780170354233

4 Sam has another thought. He realises that if he places his pen in the corner of his property against two existing fences, he might be able to build a pen each for the pigs and one for his chickens. If he just uses his original 48 m of fencing, calculate the dimensions of the total enclosure which result in a maximum total area, and calculate this area.

Step 1:

existing fence

chickens pig pig

existing fence

Step 2:

Step 3:

Step 4:

Step 5:

Step 6:

Step 7:

Step 8:

ISBN: 9780170354233

5 Let the sum of two numbers be 15. Use calculus to find the values of the numbers which make the sum of their squares a minimum.

ISBN: 9780170354233

6 An open box (no lid) is constructed from a square piece of cardboard, with a side length of 48 cm. It is made by cutting a square with a side x from each corner of the piece of cardboard. Then the remaining strips are folded up and fixed to form the sides of the box. Calculate the dimensions and volume of the box which has the biggest capacity.

ISBN: 9780170354233

7 A cylinder has a surface area of 24 cm^2. Show that its height is given by the expression $h = \frac{12 - \pi r^2}{\pi r}$. Find the radius of the cylinder which produces a maximum volume, and calculate the volume.

 ISBN: 9780170354233

8 The radius and the height of a cylinder must add to 18 cm. Calculate its maximum volume, and the values for the radius and height which produce this maximum.

ISBN: 9780170354233

Anti-differentiation

Anti-differentiating a polynomial

The rule:

Let $\frac{dy}{dx} = ax^b$.

1 Add one to the exponent: $b + 1$
Write this as the new exponent.

2 Divide the constant by the new exponent: $\frac{a}{b+1}$
Write this as the new coefficient.

So $\frac{dy}{dx} = ax^b \longrightarrow y = \frac{a}{b+1}x^{b+1}$

or $f'(x) = ax^b \longrightarrow f(x) = \frac{a}{b+1}x^{b+1}$

3 If there are several terms, just anti-differentiate each separately.

Some tricks:

1 x^2 means $1x^2$, so $f'(x) = x^2 \longrightarrow f(x) = \frac{1}{3}x^3$ or $\frac{x^3}{3}$

2 x means x^1, so $f'(x) = 7x \longrightarrow f(x) = \frac{7}{2}x^2$ or $\frac{7x^2}{2}$

3 $4 = 4x^0$, so $f'(x) = 4 \longrightarrow f(x) = \frac{4}{1}x^1 = 4x$

Examples:

1 $\frac{dy}{dx} = 15x^2 \longrightarrow y = 5x^3$

2 $f'(x) = -1 \longrightarrow f(x) = -x$

3 $\frac{dy}{dx} = 5x^4 + 2 \longrightarrow y = x^5 + 2x$

ISBN: 9780170354233

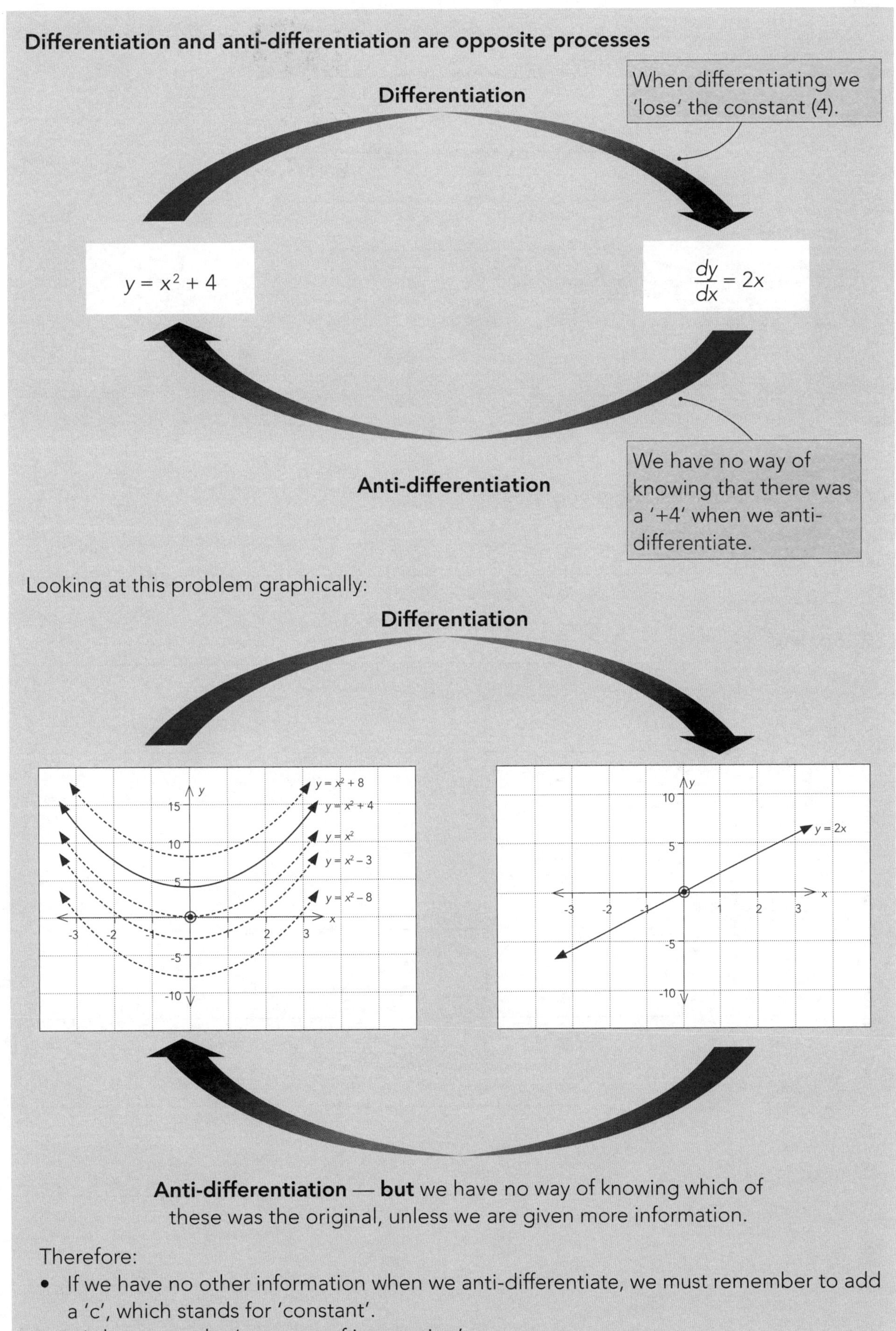

Therefore:

- If we have no other information when we anti-differentiate, we must remember to add a 'c', which stands for 'constant'.
- c is known as the 'constant of integration'.
- We are often given additional information which enables us to calculate c.

So $\frac{dy}{dx} = ax^b \longrightarrow y = \frac{a}{b+1}x^{b+1} + c$

or $f'(x) = ax^b \longrightarrow f(x) = \frac{a}{b+1}x^{b+1} + c$

Examples:

1 $\frac{dy}{dx} = 15x^2 \longrightarrow y = 5x^3 + c$

2 $f'(x) = -1 \longrightarrow f(x) = -x + c$

3 $\frac{dy}{dx} = 5x^4 + 2 \longrightarrow y = x^5 + 2x + c$

Anti-differentiate the following polynomials.

1 $\frac{dy}{dx} = 8x^3$ ________________

2 $f'(x) = x^2$ ________________

3 $\frac{dy}{dx} = -6x^5$ ________________

4 $f'(x) = 10$ ________________

5 $\frac{dy}{dx} = 23x$ ________________

6 $f'(x) = 27x^8 + 10x$ ________________

7 $\frac{dy}{dx} = 6x^5 + 4x - 2$ ________________

8 $g'(x) = 7 - 0.25x$ ________________

9 $\frac{dy}{dx} = -8 - 2x + 0.3x^2$ ________________

10 $f'(x) = x^3 - 8x^2 + 22x - 4$ ________________

ISBN: 9780170354233

Calculating c

1 Given a point on the original curve

Example one: Find the function for which $\frac{dy}{dx} = 2x$, and which passes through the point (1, 6).

Step 1: Anti-differentiate: $y = x^2 + c$

Step 2: Substitute for x and y: $6 = (1)^2 + c$

$\therefore c = 5$

Step 3: Substitute for c: $y = x^2 + 5$

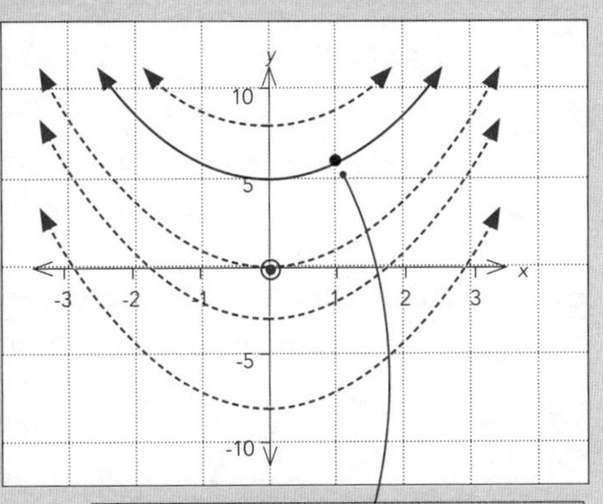

This is the only curve which passes through (1, 6)

You do not need to draw the graph to solve these.

Example two: Find the equation of the curve whose differential is $f'(x) = 6x^2 + 8x - 6$ and which passes through the point (-1,8).

Step 1: Anti-differentiate: $f(x) = 2x^3 + 4x^2 - 6x + c$

Step 2: Substitute for x and y: $8 = 2(-1)^3 + 4(-1)^2 - 6(-1) + c$

$8 = -2 + 4 + 6 + c$

$\therefore c = 0$

Step 3: Substitute for c: $f(x) = 2x^3 + 4x^2 - 6x + 0$

$f(x) = 2x^3 + 4x^2 - 6x$

Example three: Find the equation of the function for which $f'(x) = 3 - 2x - x^2$ and $f(3) = -10$.

Step 1: Anti-differentiate: $f(x) = 3x - x^2 - \frac{x^3}{3} + c$

Step 2: Substitute for x and y: $-10 = 3(3) - (3)^2 - \frac{3^3}{3} + c$

$-10 = 9 - 9 - 9 + c$

$\therefore c = -1$

Step 3: Substitute for c: $f(x) = 3x - x^2 - \frac{x^3}{3} - 1$

ISBN: 9780170354233

Find the equations for the following functions.

1 Find the function whose gradient function is $\frac{dy}{dx} = -2x$ and which passes through the point (2, 1).

2 A function passes through the point (1, 14) and has the gradient function $\frac{dy}{dx} = 8x + 7$. Find the equation of the function.

3 The gradient of a function is given by the expression $-2x + 2$. The function passes through the point (0, 2). Find the function.

4 If $g'(x) = 3x^2 - 5$, and the function passes through the point (3, 16), find the function $g(x)$.

5 For a function f, $f'(x) = 2x + 6$. The graph passes through the point (-1, 4). Find the function f.

ISBN: 9780170354233

6 A straight line has a gradient of -5 and it passes through the point (-2, 7). Find its equation by using calculus.

7 When a function is differentiated the result is $\frac{dy}{dx} = 4x^3 + 2$. If the function passes through the point (1, -4), find the equation of the function.

8 The derivative of a gradient function is given by $f'(x) = 6x^2 - 2x$. If the function passes through the point (2, 13), find the equation of the function.

9 The derivative of a function is given by $\frac{dy}{dx} = -2x - 36x^2$, and the function passes through the point (1, -4). Find the equation of the function.

10 For a function h, $h'(x) = -8x^3 + 6x$. The graph passes through the point (1, 0). Find the function h.

ISBN: 9780170354233

Challenges and applications

1 A curve $f(x)$ has a minimum value of -3. Its gradient function is $f'(x) = 2x - 4$. Find $f(x)$.

2 A curve has a gradient function $\frac{dy}{dx} = 2x - 6$ and a minimum value of 4. Find the equation of the function.

3 A curve has two turning points. Its gradient function is given by $\frac{dy}{dx} = 3x^2 - 3$. The y coordinate for the left-hand turning point is 0 and that of the right-hand turning point is -4. Calculate the equation of the function.

4 A curve has two turning points. Its gradient function is given by $\frac{dy}{dx} = 3x^2 - 12x + 9$. The y coordinate for the left-hand turning point is 4 and that of the right-hand turning point is 0. Calculate the equation of the function.

ISBN: 9780170354233

5 The graph of the function $f(x)$ is on the left. The graph of its gradient function is on the right. Calculate the function $f(x)$.

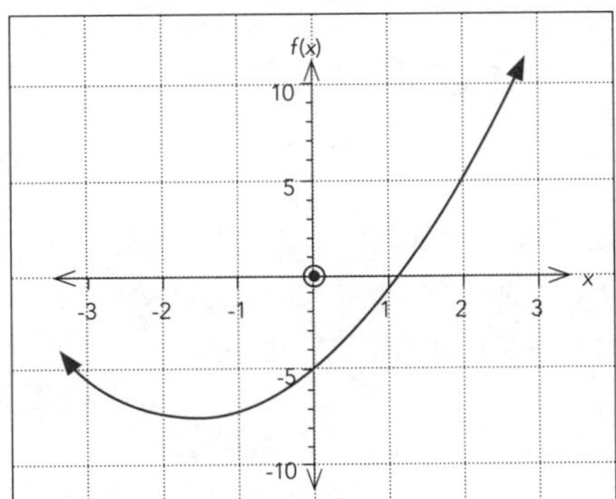

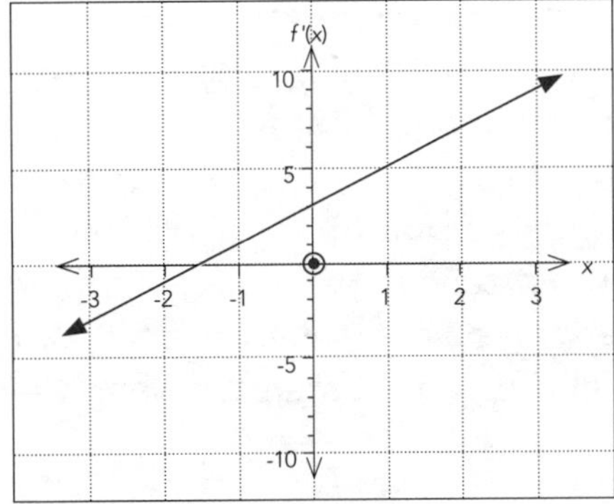

---

6 The graph of the function $g(x)$ is on the left. The graph of its gradient function is on the right. Calculate the function $g(x)$.

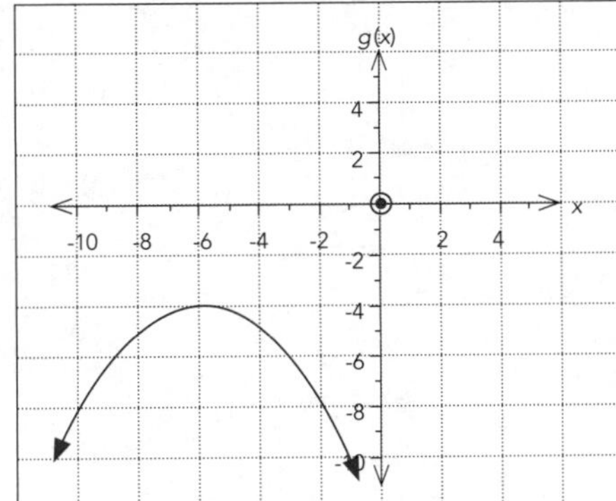

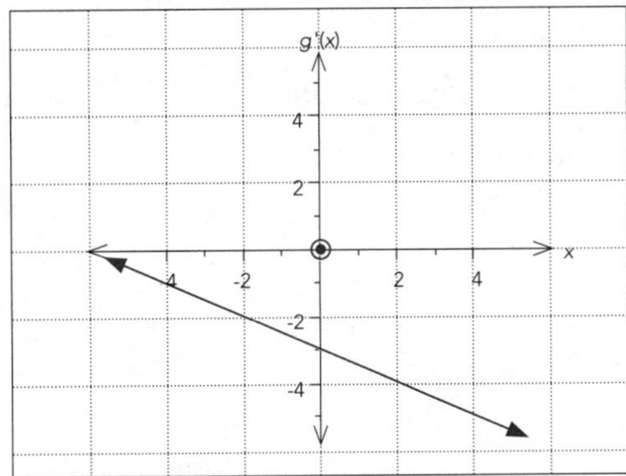

---

7 The graph of the function $h(x)$ is on the left. The graph of its gradient function is on the right. Calculate the function $h(x)$.

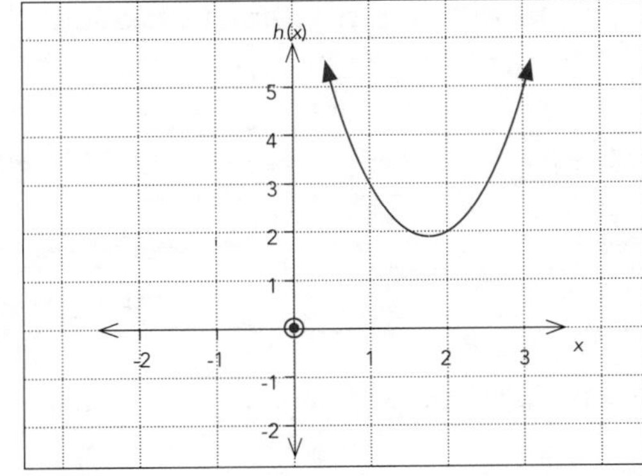

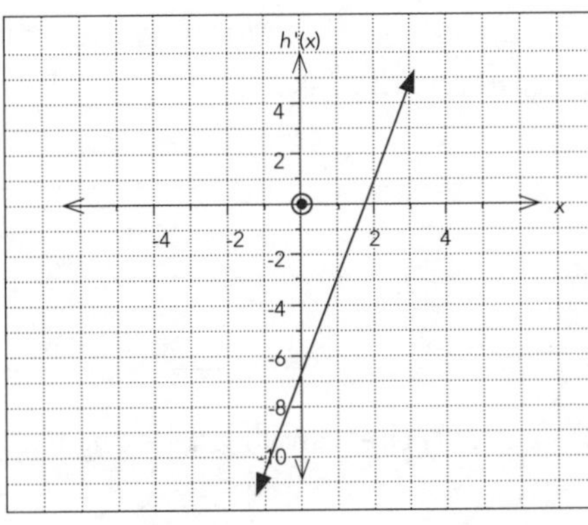

ISBN: 9780170354233

2 Given a point in a rate of change problem

This involves combining what you know about practical applications and what you already know about anti-differentiation, but:

- Instead of a **point** through which a curve passes, you will be told a **pair** of values from the practical context. For example: After 10 seconds the flow was ...
- Often the pair of values given is for the starting amount. If this is the case, then $t = 0$.
- 'Initially' means at the start when $t = 0$.

Example: A vase is left under a dripping tap. The rate at which the height of water in the vase (mm) is changing after t minutes is given by $\frac{dH}{dt} = 0.6t + 0.4$. If there was one centimetre of water in the vase to begin with, find an expression relating the height of water in the vase to the length of time since it was put there. How deep was the water after 10 minutes?

Step 1: Anti-differentiate the function: $H = 0.3t^2 + 0.4t + c$

Step 2: Find c: substitute $H = 10$ and $t = 0$:
$1 = 0.3(0)^2 + 0.4(0) + c$
$c = 10$

$\therefore H = 0.3t^2 + 0.4t + 10$

Step 3: Substitute $t = 10$:
$H = 0.3(10)^2 + 0.4(10) + 10$
$H = 44$ mm

$\therefore$ After 10 minutes there will be 44 mm of water in the vase.

Solve the following problems.

1 Diesel is leaking from a tank on a fishing boat. Before the leak began, the tank had just been filled with 2900 L of diesel. The change in the volume of diesel (V) in the tank after t hours is given by the expression $\frac{dV}{dt} = -52 + 0.4t$.

a Find an expression relating the volume of diesel left in the tank to the length of time after the leak began.

b How much diesel will be left in the tank after 20 hours?

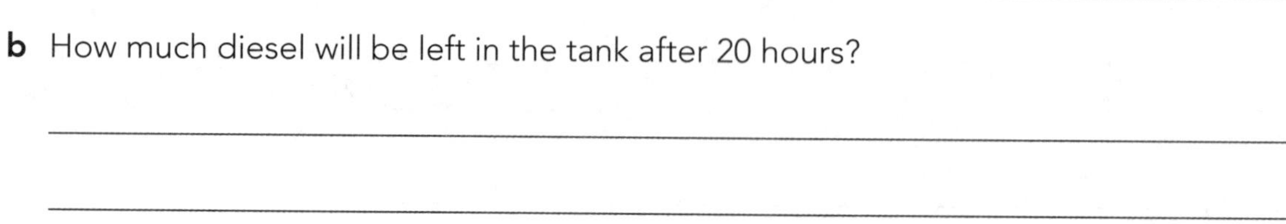

 ISBN: 9780170354233

2 The rate at which a slow-growing population of animals is predicted to increase with time (years) is $P'(t) = t - 0.012t^2$. If there were 50 animals to start with:

a Find an expression for $P(t)$.

b Calculate the number of animals after 10 years.

3 Edward bought a painting for $1000. The rate at which its value (V) changes is given by $\frac{dV}{dt} = 24t + 20$, where t represents time in years since he bought it.

a Find an expression which relates the painting's value to how long he has owned it.

b How much will the painting be worth in 10 years?

4 A school canteen buys a supply of 300 juice ice blocks. They become increasingly popular with the students and staff during a hot spell of weather. A canteen helper works out that the stock of ice blocks is changing at a rate of ($-5 - 4t$) per day.

a Find an expression which relates the number of ice blocks to the number of days after they started to sell them.

b How many ice blocks are left by day 11?

ISBN: 9780170354233

5 Keri is winding knitting wool into a ball. The change in the weight of wool in the ball is proportional to the radius of the ball and this is given by the relationship $\frac{dW}{dr} = 0.24r^2$. The weight of wool (W) is in grams and the radius of the ball (r) is in centimetres.

a If she started with nothing, find an expression which relates the radius of the ball to its weight.

b How heavy will the ball be when its radius is 6 cm?

6 A fishpond is being filled by a pipe in its base. The volume (V) of water in it depends on how many minutes (t) the valve in the pipe has been left open. The rate of flow into the pond is given by $\frac{dV}{dt} = 4t - 0.1$. After 10 minutes the volume of water in the pond is 210 L.

a Find an expression which relates the volume of water in the pond to the length of time the valve has been left open.

b How much water will be in the pond after 20 minutes?

7 A patient with a dangerously high temperature of 41°C is given a drug which will reduce his temperature (T) over a period of hours (h). The rate at which his temperature is dropping is given by the expression $T'(h) = -0.04 - 0.02h$.

a Find an expression which relates the patient's temperature to the length of time he has been taking the drug.

b Calculate his expected temperature 10 hours after starting to take the drug.

ISBN: 9780170354233

3 Using a graph of the gradient function to sketch the original curve

If you are given the **graph** of the gradient function and the **coordinates of a point** on the graph of the function, you can sketch the function.

Points to remember:

- The gradient function crosses the x-axis in line with the turning point ($\frac{dy}{dx} = 0$).
- Parabolas are symmetrical.
- c represents the *y* intercept.
- You may not be told the coordinates of the point explicitly. For example, you may be told a maximum or a minimum value (the *y* coordinate), and the x coordinate will be where the gradient function crosses the x-axis.

Example: Sketch the function $f(x)$ for the gradient function $f'(x)$ which is drawn below. The function passes through the point (5, 6).

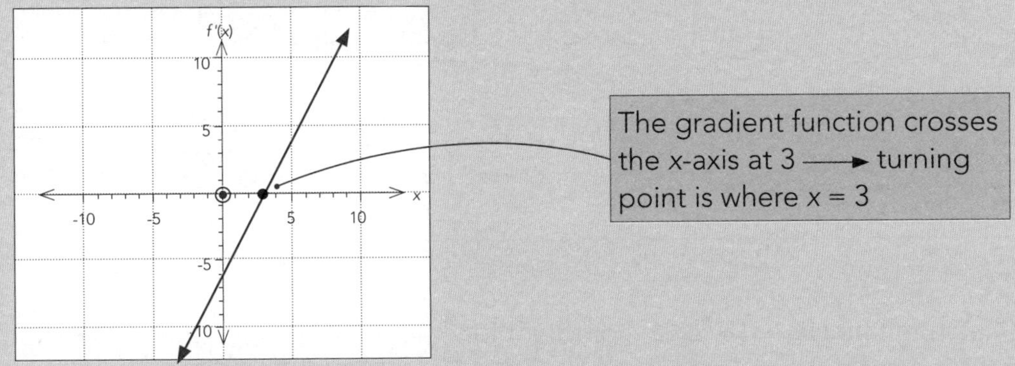

Step 1: Write the equation: $f'(x) = 2x - 6$

Step 2: Anti-differentiate: $f(x) = x^2 - 6x + c$

Step 3: Substitute (5, 6) to find c: $6 = (5)^2 - 6(5) + c$

$c = 11$

$\therefore f(x) = x^2 - 6x + 11$

Remember c represents the *y* intercept.

Step 4: Calculate the minimum value: $f(x) = (3)^2 - 6(3) + 11$

$f(x) = 2$

f(x)
15
10
5
-10
-5
5
10
x
-5

y intercept

Symmetrical with (0, 11)

Minimum

Sketch the following functions using the information given.

1 Sketch the function $f(x)$ for the gradient function $f'(x)$ shown below, given that the function passes through the point (3, 7).

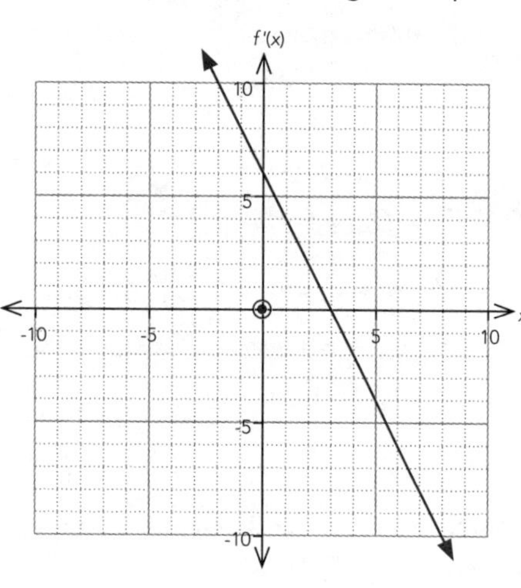

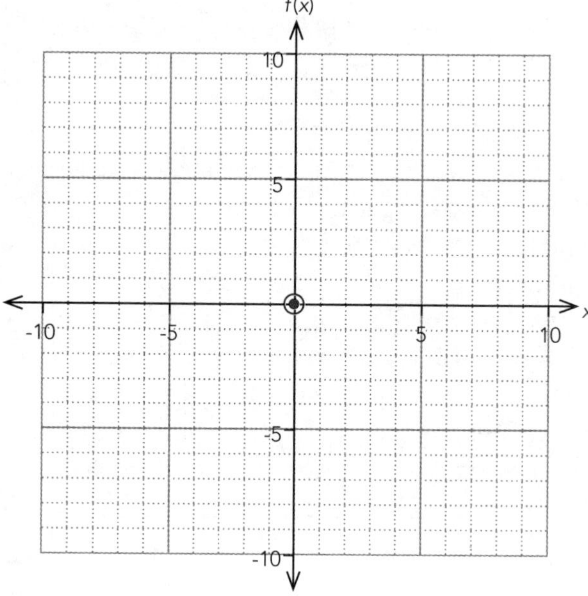

2 Sketch the function $f(x)$ for the gradient function $f'(x)$ shown below, given that the function has a minimum value of -7.

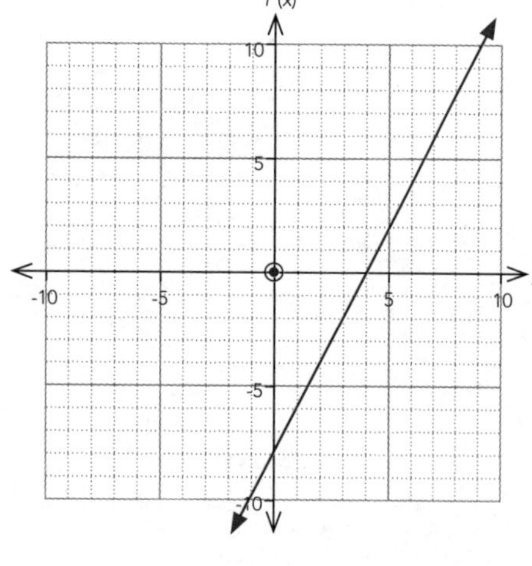

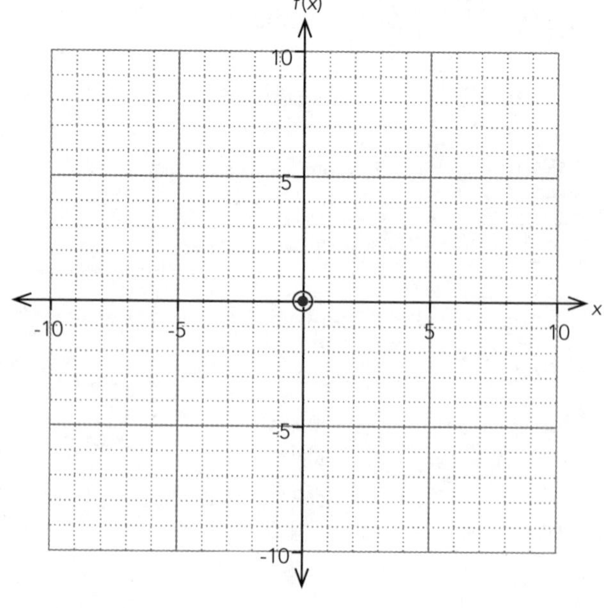

ISBN: 9780170354233

3 Sketch the function $f(x)$ for the gradient function $f'(x)$ shown below, given that the function passes through the point (-1, 3).

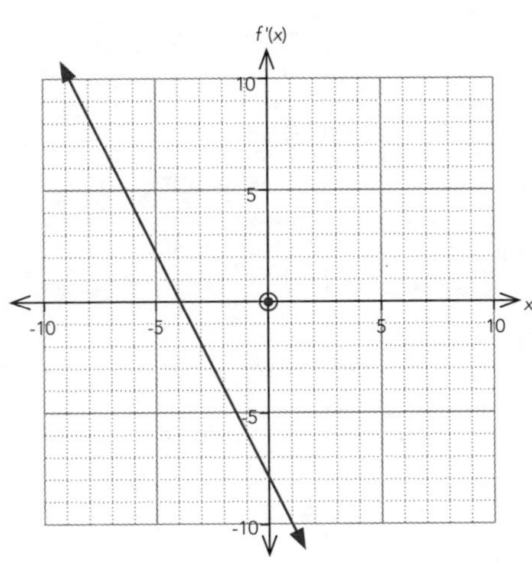

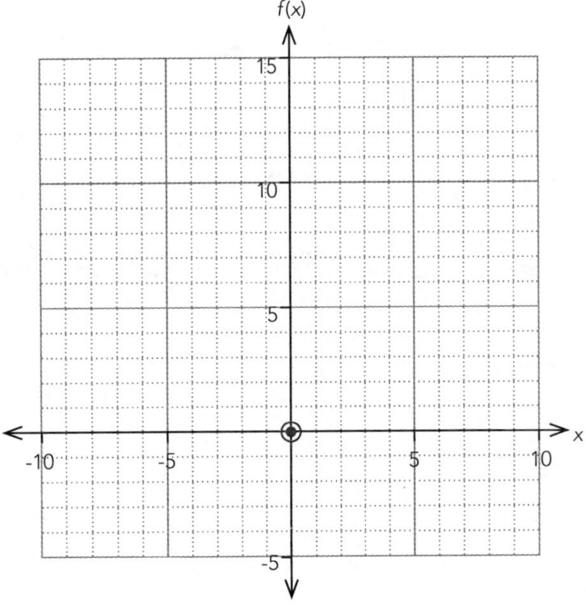

4 Sketch the function $f(x)$ for the gradient function $f'(x)$ shown below, given that the function passes through the point (-2, 9).

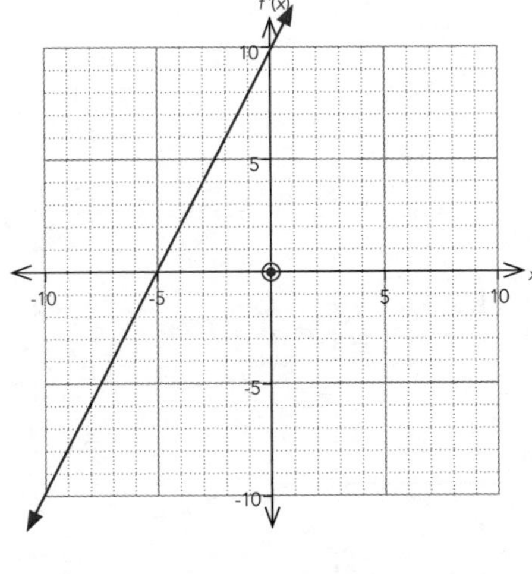

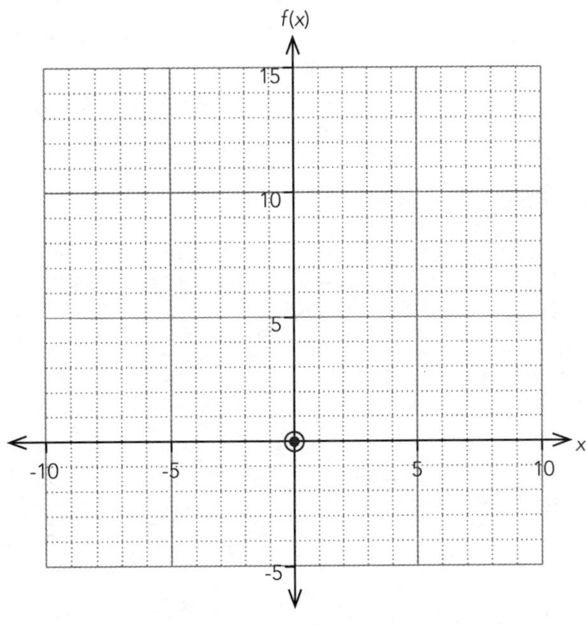

ISBN: 9780170354233

5 Sketch the function $f(x)$ for the gradient function $f'(x)$ shown below, given that the function passes through the origin.

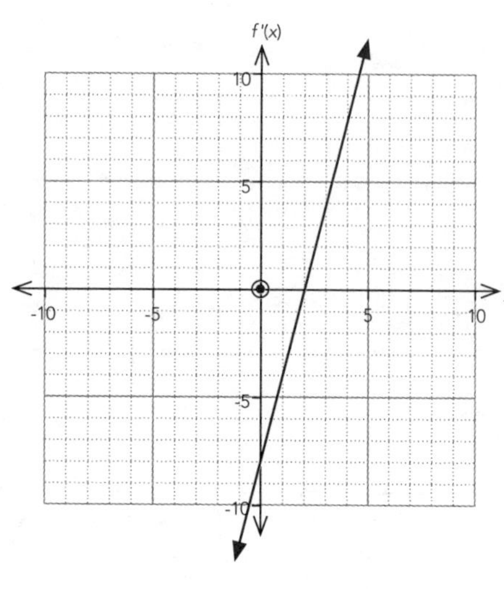

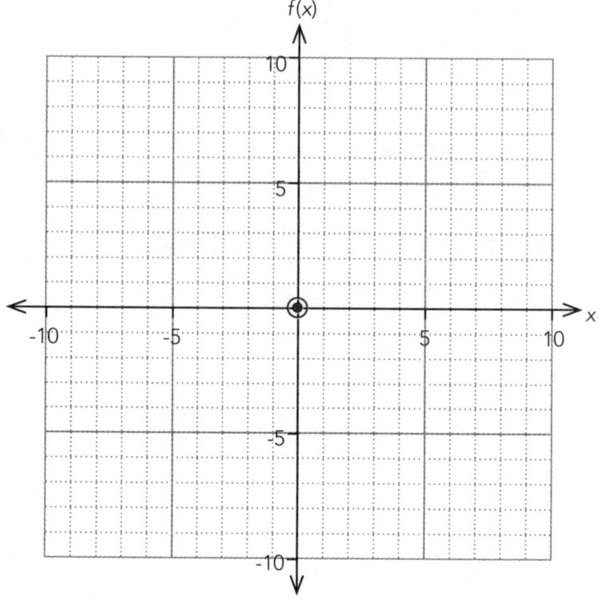

6 Sketch the function $f(x)$ for the gradient function $f'(x)$ shown below, given that the function has a maximum value of 7.

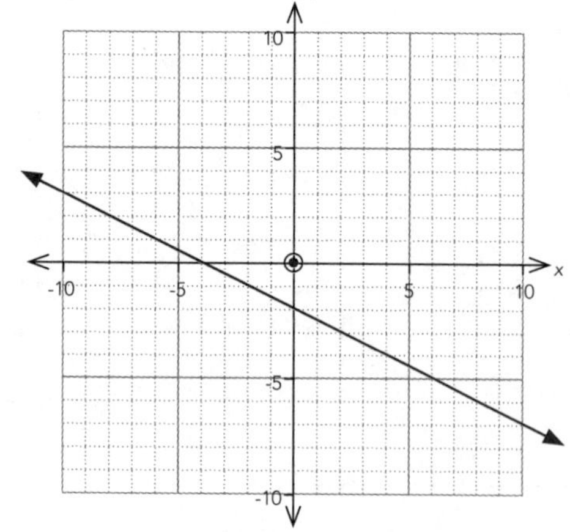

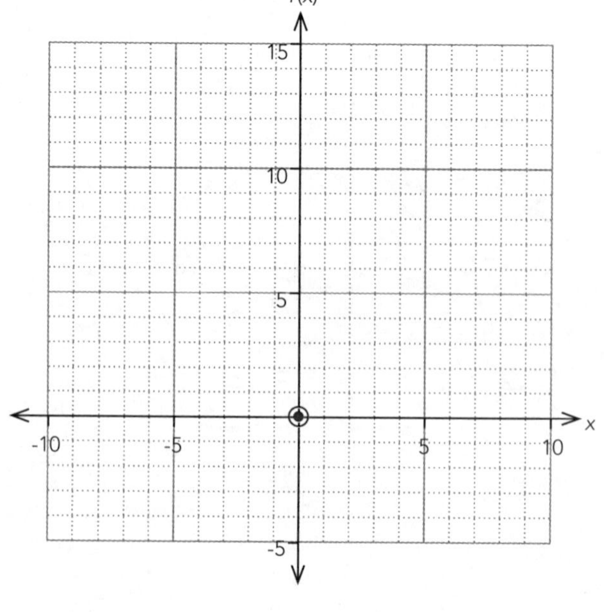

ISBN: 9780170354233

Kinematics

Introduction and terminology

Kinematics is the study of motion.

Parameters and units

Letter	What it stands for	Unit
t	time	seconds (s)
s	distance	metres (m)
v	velocity = change in distance with respect to time $= \frac{ds}{dt} = v(t) = s'(t)$	metres/second (m/s)
a	acceleration = change in velocity with respect to time $= \frac{dv}{dt} = a(t) = v'(t) = \frac{d_2s}{dt^2}$	metres per second per second (m/s^2)

Terminology for differentiating a second time

Conventions and terms

- All motion is considered to start from the origin. It is usually horizontal, but if it is vertical then the origin is ground level.
- Motion usually starts where time = 0. 'Initially' ⟶ $t = 0$.
- Velocity = 0 if the object is 'at rest', 'at its greatest height', or 'stopped'.
  Units: distance/time, e.g. m/s, m/min, km/h.
- Acceleration: +ve ⟶ object is speeding up
  –ve ⟶ object is slowing down
  = 0 ⟶ object is at a constant speed.
  Units: distance/time^2, e.g. m/s^2, m/min^2, km/h^2.
- 'When' ⟶ find the time.
- 'Where' ⟶ find the distance.

Because these interrelationships involve change, we can apply our calculus skills:

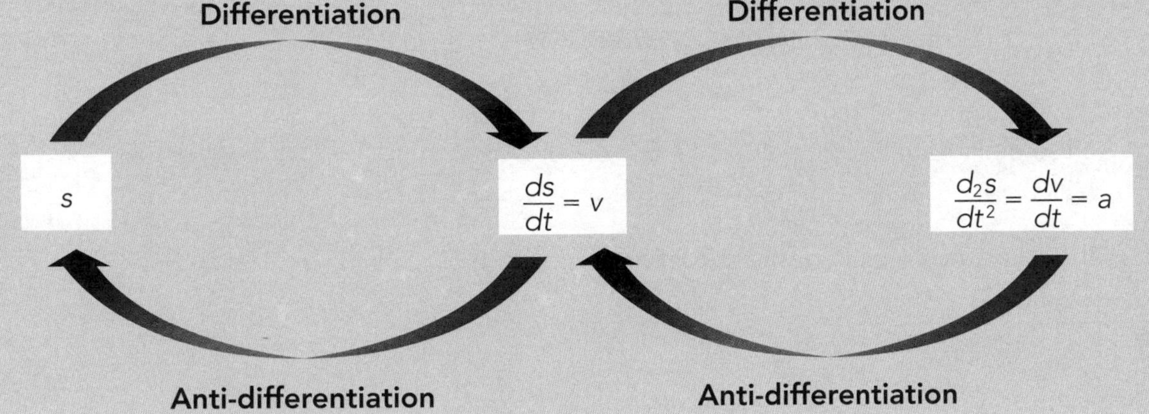

Differentiation in kinematics

These problems may involve:

- using a given relationship to calculate the distance travelled during an interval
- differentiating to find velocity or acceleration
- maximum or minimum height, distance or velocity
- when an object has a given velocity or acceleration.

Example: A rocket is fired into the air. The relationship between its height, h (in metres), above the ground and the time, t (in seconds), since it was launched is given by $h = 1 + 60t - 4t^2$.

a How far above the ground was the rocket when it was launched?

At the time it was launched, $t = 0 \therefore h = 1 + 60(0) - 4(0)^2$

$h = 1$

So the rocket was launched from 1 m above the ground.

b How far did the rocket travel during the first second of its flight?

$t = 0 \longrightarrow h = 1$

$t = 1 \longrightarrow h = 1 + 60(1) - 4(1)^2$

$h = 57$ m

$\therefore$ The rocket travels 57 – 1 = 56 m during the first second.

c How fast was the rocket travelling after 2 seconds?

$v = \frac{dh}{dt} = 60 - 8t$

$t = 2 \longrightarrow v = 60 - 8(2)$

$v = 44$ m/s

d Calculate the rocket's acceleration after 2 seconds.

$a = \frac{dv}{dt} = -8 \text{ m/s}^2$

e What was the maximum height reached by the rocket?

Maximum is reached when $v = 0 \therefore 60 - 8t = 0$

$t = 7.5$ s

So the maximum height $= 1 + 60(7.5) - 4(7.5)^2$

$= 226$ m

f When was the velocity of the rocket equal to 12 m/s?

$v = 12 \longrightarrow 60 - 8t = 12$

$t = 6$ s

$\therefore$ After 6 seconds.

ISBN: 9780170354233

Try these questions.

1 Alison throws a stone vertically into the air. The relationship between the height of the stone (h) in metres and the time (t) in seconds since she threw it is given by $h = 2 + 20t - 5t^2$.

a How far above the ground was the stone when it left her hand?

b How far did the stone travel during the first second of its flight?

c How fast was the stone travelling after 1 second?

d Calculate the stone's acceleration after 1 second.

e Calculate the stone's maximum height.

f When was the velocity of the stone equal to 12 m/s?

ISBN: 9780170354233

2 The distance (in metres) travelled by a vintage car after t seconds is given by the relationship $s = 0.2t^2 + 3t$.

a How far has it travelled after 4 seconds?

b Calculate its velocity after 4 seconds.

c When was its velocity 9 m/s?

d Calculate the acceleration of the car.

3 A stone is dropped into a well. The relationship between the time since it was dropped and the distance it has travelled is given by $s = 5t^2$, where distance is measured in metres and time in seconds.

a What is the velocity of the stone after 2 seconds?

b How far has the stone dropped after 2 seconds?

c If the stone was travelling at 29.7 m/s when it hit the water, how deep was the well?

ISBN: 9780170354233

4 The distance (in metres) travelled by a train from a station is given by the relationship $s = 2t^2 - \frac{t^3}{9}$, where t stands for time in seconds.

a How far has it travelled after 2 seconds?

b How fast is it travelling after 2 seconds?

c Calculate the acceleration of the train after 2 seconds.

d When was the train travelling fastest? How far was the train from the station when this occurred?

e When did the train return to the station?

f When was the train the greatest distance from the station? How far was it from the station?

ISBN: 9780170354233

5 Phoebe plays bowls. The distance she bowls is given by the relationship $s = 12t - 2t^2$ for $0 < t < 3$ seconds. The distance is in metres.

a How far does her bowl travel in the first 2 seconds?

b How fast is her bowl travelling after 2 seconds?

c When does her bowl stop?

d How far did her bowl travel overall?

e Calculate the acceleration of the bowl. Explain what this means.

f Why does the equation apply to her bowl only when $0 < t < 3$ seconds?

ISBN: 9780170354233

Anti-differentiation in kinematics

1 Anti-differentiating once to calculate c

a: Given the velocity, calculate the distance

In kinematics you are sometimes given an expression for the velocity, and you need to work backwards to find a distance, so:

- In order to find an expression for distance you need the coordinates of a point so that you can evaluate c.
- Often you will be told that the object starts from rest. This tells you two points:
  1 When $t = 0$, $s = 0$.
  2 When $t = 0$, $v = 0$.
- Sometimes the context will indirectly tell you a point, e.g. if an object is thrown, then at the instant before it is thrown, $t = 0$, $v = 0$ and $s = 0$.

You might find it useful to sketch the diagram:

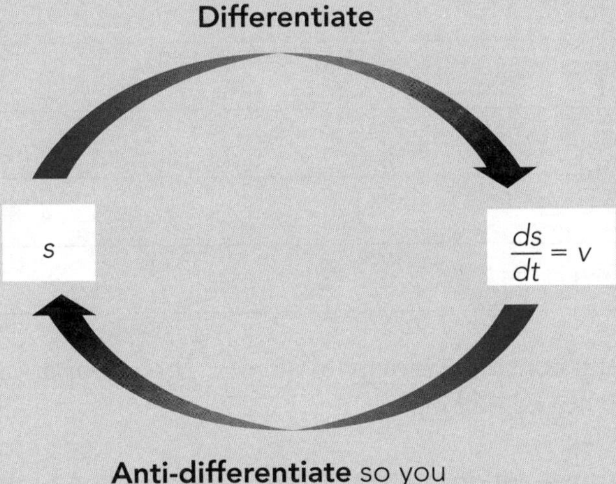

Example: A sky rocket is fired vertically into the air from the roof of a 60 m building. Its velocity is given by $v = 50 - 10t$, where velocity is given in m/s.

Calculate its vertical height after 2 seconds.

Step 1: Anti-differentiate $v \longrightarrow s$: $s = 50t - 5t^2 + c$

Step 2: Substitute for $t = 0$ and $s = 60$: $s = 50(0) - 5(0)^2 + c = 60$

$\therefore c = 60$

so $s = 50t - 5t^2 + 60$

Step 3: Substitute $t = 2$: $s = 50(2) - 5(2)^2 + 60$

$s = 140$ m

After the 2 seconds, the sky rocket is 140 m high.

ISBN: 9780170354233

Try these questions.

1 A rocket is fired vertically from the ground. The relationship between its velocity in m/s and the time since it was fired is given by $v = 100 - 10t$. Calculate the height of the rocket after 2 seconds.

2 A weather balloon is released from ground level. It rises at a velocity of $3 - 0.2t$ km/h. How high will it be after 2 hours?

3 A car is travelling at a constant velocity of 28 m/s. The driver applies the brakes and changes the velocity to $28 - 2t$ m/s.

a How far will he travel during the first 10 seconds after the brakes are applied?

b When will the car stop?

c After what distance does it stop?

  ISBN: 9780170354233

4 A rock is dropped into a deep cave. The relationship between the distance it has dropped, in m, and velocity is given by $v = 9.8t$. If the rock took 3.2 seconds to reach the bottom, calculate its depth.

5 A Martian (on Mars) drops a rock into a cave from 2 m above ground level. The relationship between the distance it has dropped and velocity is given by $v = 3.7t$. If his rock also took 3.2 seconds to reach the bottom, calculate the depth of the Martian cave.

6 The velocity of a toy car is given by the relationship $v = 18 - 0.06t^2$ cm/s.

a How long will it take before it stops?

b How far will it go before it stops?

7 Hine is cycling at a constant velocity of 10 m/s. She speeds up and maintains a steady velocity of $10 + 0.2t$ m/s for 30 seconds. Calculate how far she travels during the 30 seconds.

b: Given the acceleration, calculate the velocity

Alternatively, you could be given an expression for the acceleration, and you need to work backwards to find a velocity. Once again, in order to find an expression for velocity, you need the coordinates of a point so that you can evaluate c.

You might find it useful to sketch the diagram:

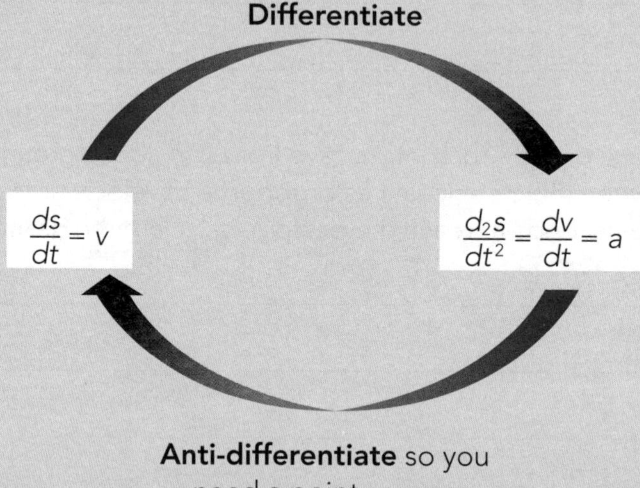

Example: A snowboarder begins to move down a slope with an acceleration given by $a = 0.36t^2 + 2$. Calculate the velocity of the snowboarder after 5 seconds.

Step 1: Anti-differentiate $a \longrightarrow v$: $v = 0.12t^3 + 2t + c$

Step 2: Substitute for $t = 0$ and $v = 0$: $v = 0.12(0)^3 + 2(0) + c = 0$
$\therefore$ c = 0
so $v = 0.12t^3 + 2t$

Step 3: Substitute $t = 5$: $v = 0.12(5)^3 + 2(5)$
$v = 25$ m/s

So after 5 seconds the snowboarder is travelling at 25 m/s.

Try these questions.

1 A builder accidentally drops his hammer from the top of a five-storey building. The hammer accelerates at 9.8 m/s^2. It hits the ground 1.8 seconds later. Calculate the velocity of the hammer when it hits the ground.

ISBN: 9780170354233

2 A stationary bus accelerates for 5 seconds at $0.8t$ m/s^2. Calculate its velocity at the end of this period.

3 A ball is thrown vertically into the air. Its acceleration is -9.8 m/s^2. If its initial velocity is 12 m/s:

a When does it reach its maximum height?

b Calculate its velocity after 1 second.

4 A rowing eight is moving at a constant velocity of 6 m/s and coming second in its race. In order to try to win, they accelerate at a rate of $0.06t$. How fast will they be rowing after accelerating at this rate for 5 seconds?

5 At the start of a race a sprinter accelerates at 2.1 m/s^2. For how long will he need to sustain this rate of acceleration in order to reach his maximum speed of 4 m/s?

ISBN: 9780170354233

2 Anti-differentiating twice to calculate c and c' — given the acceleration, calculate the distance

In kinematics you are sometimes given an expression for the acceleration and you need to work backwards to find a distance, so:

- In order to find an expression for velocity you need the coordinates of a point so that you can evaluate c.
- In order to find an expression for distance you need the coordinates of another point so that you can evaluate c′.
- Often you will be told that the object starts from rest. This tells you two points:
  1 When $t = 0$, $s = 0$.
  2 When $t = 0$, $v = 0$.

Because you will need to anti-differentiate twice, it is a good idea to sketch this diagram:

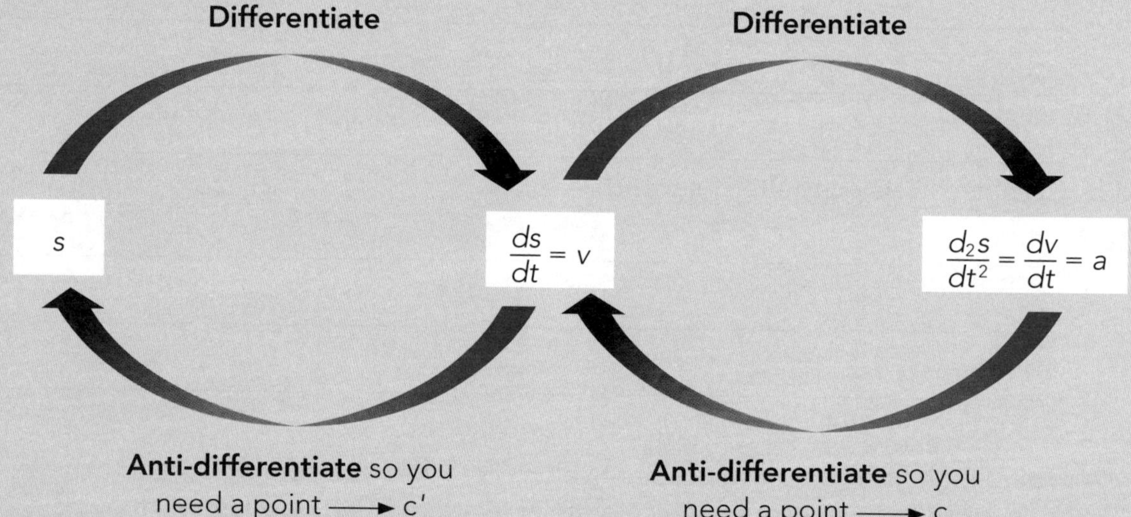

Example: A car is initially moving at 10 m/s. It accelerates at a constant rate of 2 m/s^2 for 4 seconds. How far did it travel during the 4 seconds?

Step 1: Anti-differentiate $a \longrightarrow v$: $a = 2$ m/s$^2 \longrightarrow v = 2t + c$

Step 2: Substitute $t = 0$ and $v(0) = 10$

$v = 2(0) + c = 10$
$\therefore$ c = 10
so $v = 2t + 10$

Step 3: Anti-differentiate $v \longrightarrow s$: $s = t^2 + 10t + c'$

Step 4: Substitute for $t = 0$ and $s = 0$:

$s = (0)^2 + 10(0) + c' = 0$
$\therefore c' = 0$
so $s = t^2 + 10t$

Step 5: Substitute $t = 4$:

$s = (4)^2 + 10(4)$
$s = 56$ m

So during the 4 seconds, the car travels 56 m.

ISBN: 9780170354233

Try these questions.

1 An electronic toy truck accelerates at 0.6 m/s^2 when it is switched on. How far will it travel in its first minute?

2 A car which is travelling at 30 m/s (108 km/h) is signalled to stop by a police officer. When the driver applies the brakes he decelerates at 2 m/s^2 ($a = -2 \text{ m/s}^2$).

a How long does it take him to stop?

b How far does he travel between the time he applies his brakes and the time he stops?

3 A truck is being driven along a straight road at a constant velocity of 15 m/s. It accelerates at $\frac{t}{10} - 2 \text{ m/s}^2$. Calculate how far it will travel during the first minute of acceleration.

ISBN: 9780170354233

4 A car is travelling at a constant velocity of 22.2 m/s (80 km/h) when it comes to a derestriction sign so the driver increases its speed to 27.8 m/s (100 km/h). Its acceleration during this period is given by $a = 0.06t$.

a How long does it take to accelerate from 22.2 m/s to 27.8 m/s?

b Calculate the distance required to accelerate from 22.2 m/s to 27.8 m/s.

5 An astronaut whose spaceship has landed on the moon drops a spanner from a height of 5 m above the moon's surface. Acceleration due to gravity on the moon is -1.67 m/s^2. How long does it take before the spanner lands on the moon's surface?

6 A train starts from rest. Its acceleration after t seconds is given by $a = \frac{1}{5}(10 - t)$ m/s^2. How far does the train go in the first 20 seconds?

ISBN: 9780170354233

Practice questions

Practice question one

a A function *f* is given by $f(x) = 9x^2 - 7x - 4$. Calculate the gradient of the graph where $x = 2$.

b For the function g, $g'(x) = 5 - 3x^2$. The graph passes through the point (2, 15). Find the function $g(x)$.

c A ball is thrown into the air. Its height above the ground is given by $h = 20t - 5t^2 + 2$, where t is time in seconds since the ball was thrown. What is the maximum height reached by the ball?

ISBN: 9780170354233

d The diameter of a puddle (p centimetres) under a leaky tap t hours after the leak starts is modelled by the function $p(t) = -0.2t^2 + 7t + 3$. When will the rate of increase in the diameter of the puddle be 3 cm per hour?

e $h(x) = x^3 - 12x + 5$. For what values of x is h a decreasing function? You must show the use of calculus in your working.

f The gradient of a curve is given by $\frac{dy}{dx} = -6x^2 + 12x$. The y coordinate of the maximum turning point is 1. Find the equation of the curve.

ISBN: 9780170354233

Practice question two

a Find the x coordinate of the point on the graph of $f(x) = x^2 + 7$ where the gradient is equal to 10.

b A function is given by $g(x) = x^2 + 7$. Calculate the gradients of the graph at the points where $g(x) = 16$.

c For the function h, $h'(x) = -2x + A$. This function has a maximum at the point (2, 3). Find the value of A and the equation of the function h.

d The distance, in millimetres, of a snail from its hiding place is given by $s = 1.5t^2 + 6t$, where t represents time in seconds since it left its hiding place, for $0 \leqslant t \leqslant 10$. Give the equation for the velocity of the snail, and use it to find when its velocity is 24 mm/s.

ISBN: 9780170354233

e The volume of a sphere is given by $V = \frac{4}{3}\pi r^3$, where r is its radius in centimetres. Calculate the rate of change in the volume, with respect to the radius, when the volume is 288π cm^3.

f Sketch the function $g(x)$ for the gradient function $g'(x)$ below, given that the minimum value of g is -7. Show the vertex clearly.

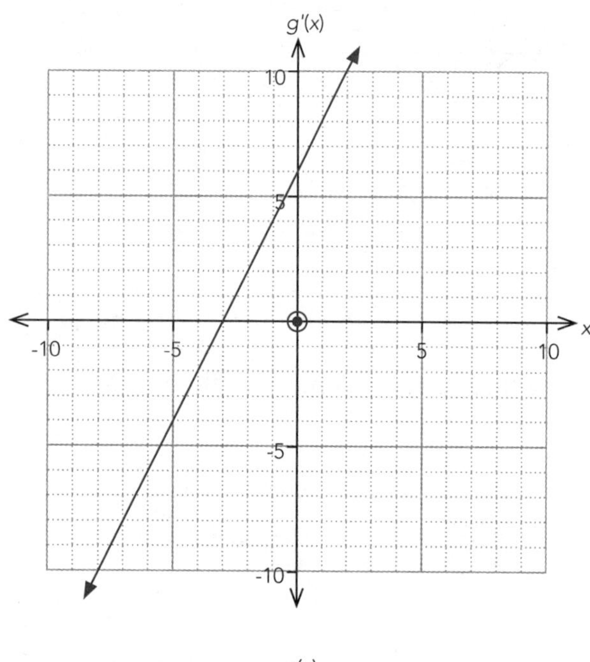

g(x)

 ISBN: 9780170354233

Practice question three

a A curve $y = f(x)$ passes through (1, 0) and has a gradient function $f'(x) = 5 - 4x$. Find the coordinates of the point where $x = -1$.

b The population of rare birds is given by the relationship $p(t) = 467 - 7t - 0.1t^3$, where t represents time in years. Calculate the rate of change of the population after 10 years.

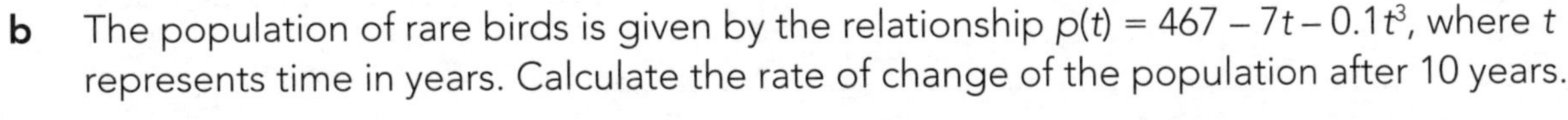

c Find the equation of the tangent to the curve $g(x) = x - 3x^2$ at the point (2, -10).

d The graph of the function $h(x)$ together with the graph of its gradient function $h'(x)$ are given below. Find the equation of $h(x)$. You must use calculus methods to obtain your answer.

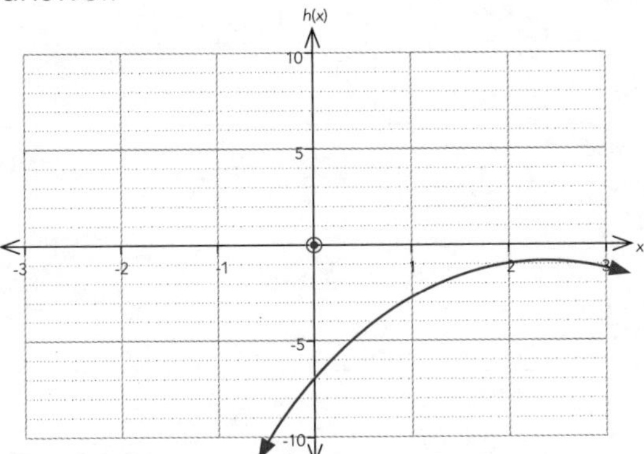

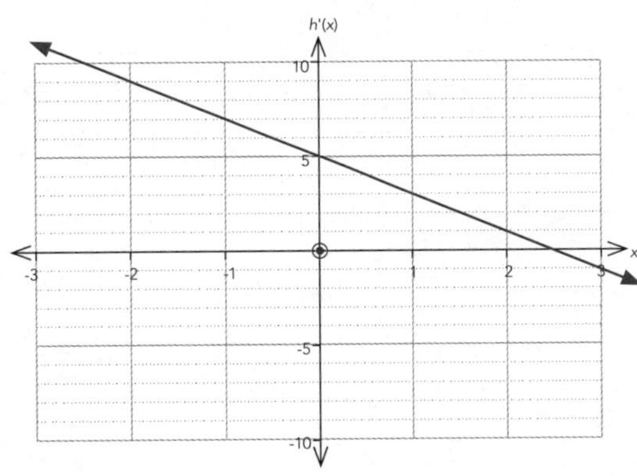

ISBN: 9780170354233

e Simon is jogging at a constant velocity of 2 m/s. At a big tree he slows down by reducing his velocity to $2 - 0.01t$ m/s. How far will he run in the first two minutes after leaving the big tree?

f An integer is doubled, and then added to a different integer to give a total of 15. Use calculus to find the values for these two integers so that the sum of their squares is a minimum.

 ISBN: 9780170354233

Practice question four

a Sketch the gradient function $f'(x)$ of the function $f(x)$ below.

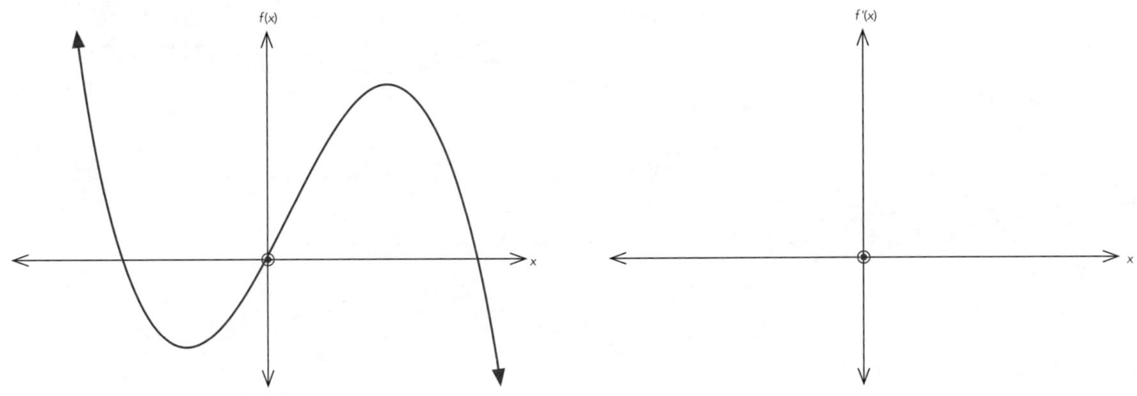

b Find the coordinates of the turning point of the function $g(x) = 5x^2 - 24x + 3$.

c Alison bought a second-hand car for $13,000. The rate at which its value changes is given by $\frac{dv}{dt} = -600 - 24t$, where v represents the car's value in dollars and t represents time in years. Calculate the value of the car after 5 years.

ISBN: 9780170354233

d A landscaper is constructing a garden which has a one-metre wall on one side. Its height is given by the relationship $h = 1 + 0.4x - \frac{x^2}{50}$, where h represents height in metres and x represents distance in metres from the wall. Show that the garden rises to a *maximum* 10 metres from the wall.

e The curve of $f(x) = -2x^3 + Ax + B$ has a tangent with a gradient of 3 at the point (1, 10). Find the coordinates of the point on the curve where $x = -1$.

f A car starts from rest. Its acceleration t seconds after it starts is given by $a = 1.6 - \frac{1}{20}t$ m/s^2. How far does it go in the first 20 seconds?

  ISBN: 9780170354233

Practice question five

a Sketch the gradient function $f'(x)$ of the function $f(x)$ below.

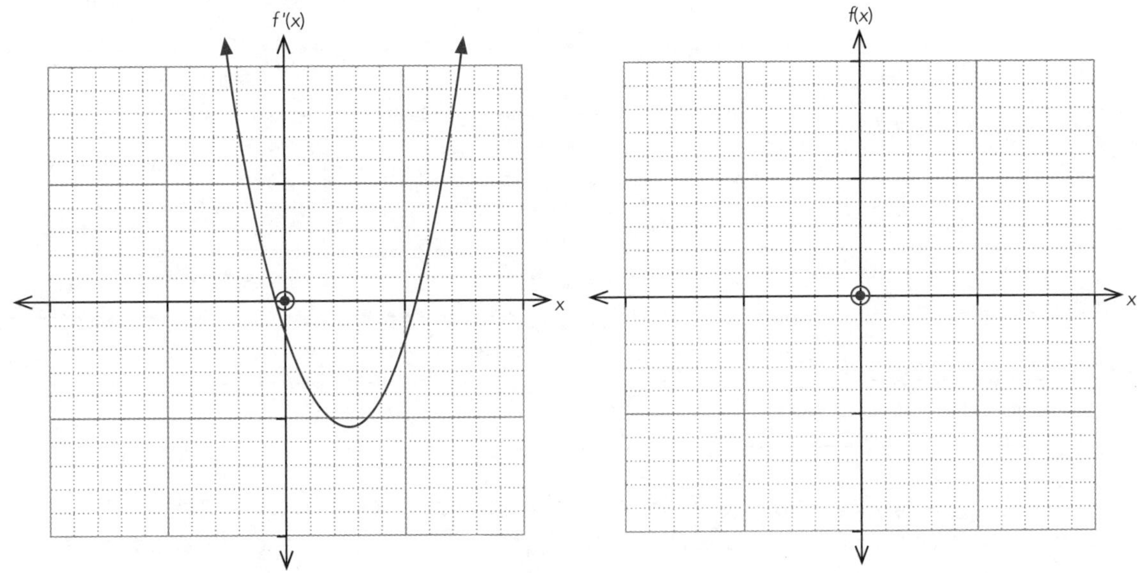

b The graph shows the gradient function for $f'(x)$. Find the equation for $f(x)$, given that $f(x)$ passes through the point (6, -15).

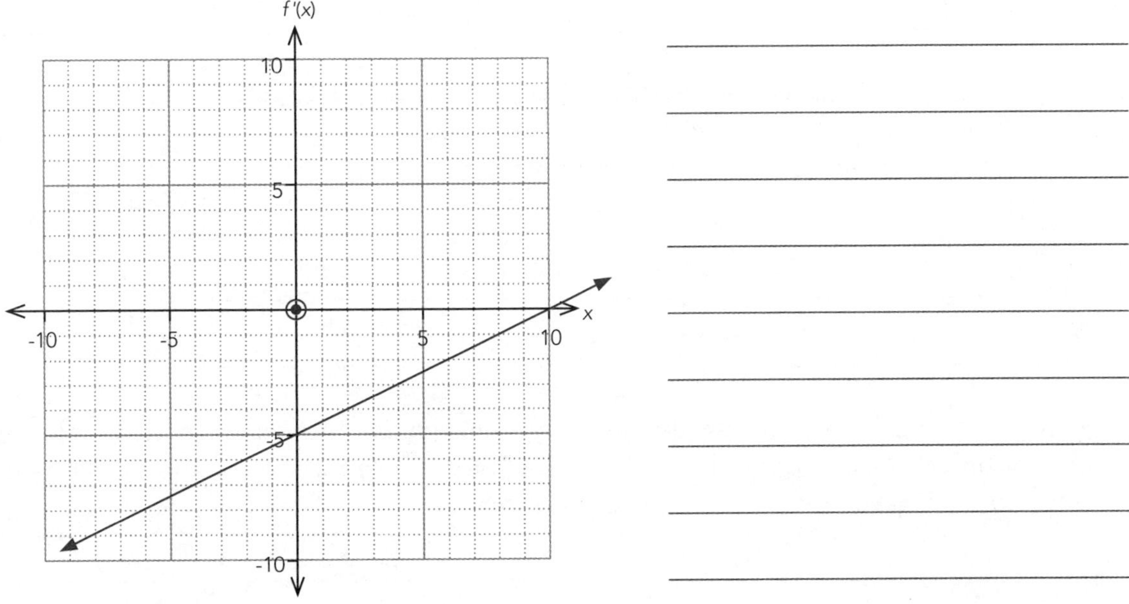

c $g(x) = x^3 - 9x^2 + 15x - 10$. For what values of x is g a decreasing function. You must justify your answer using calculus.

d The fuel consumption, f, of a scooter, in litres per 100 km, is related to the velocity, v, in km h^{-1}, by the formula $f = 5 - 0.4v + \frac{v^2}{100}$. Show that the fuel consumption is at a **minimum** when v = 20 km h^{-1}.

e An object is dropped from 20 m above the moon's surface. On the moon, acceleration due to gravity is 1.6m/s^2. How long will it take to reach the surface of the moon?

f A cone is to be constructed so that its height plus its diameter is 48cm. Calculate the maximum volume possible for the cone. The formula for the volume of a cone is $v = \frac{1}{3}\pi r^2 h$, and you may leave π in your answer.

 ISBN: 9780170354233

Answers

Answers are rounded to a maximum of 4 d.p. Professional judgement should apply.

Introduction (pp. 6–14)

Gradient revision (p. 7)

Gradient A = 2
Gradient B = -4
Gradient C = -0.2
Gradient D = 0
Gradient E = 1
Gradient F = undefined

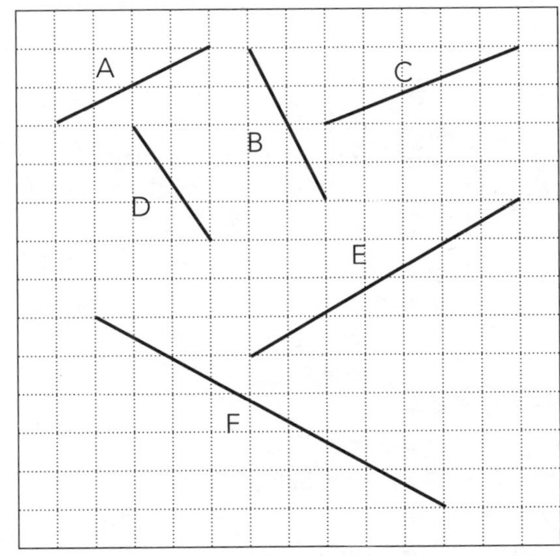

Sketching gradient functions of curves (pp. 11–12)

1

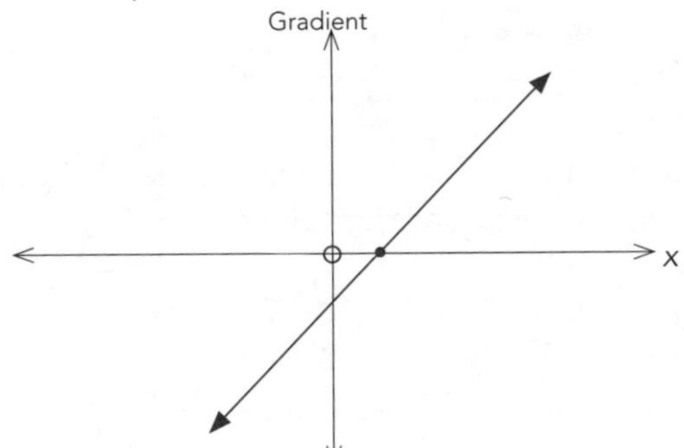

2

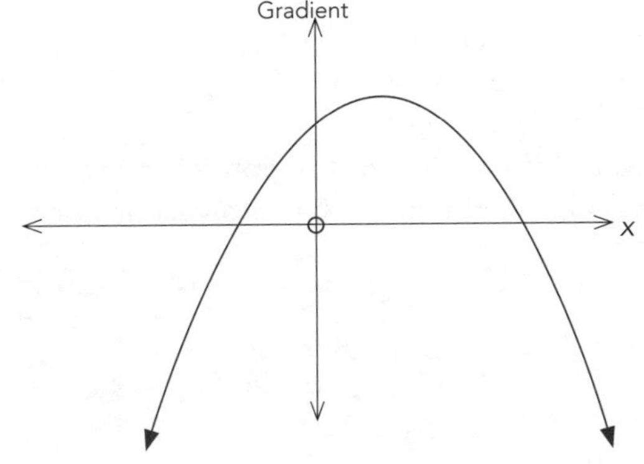

3

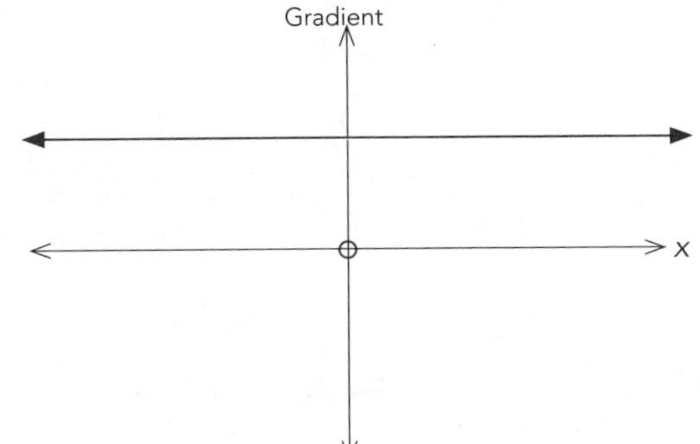

4

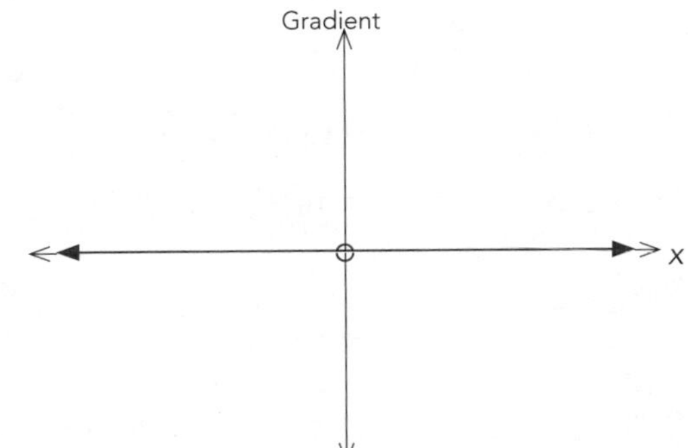

5

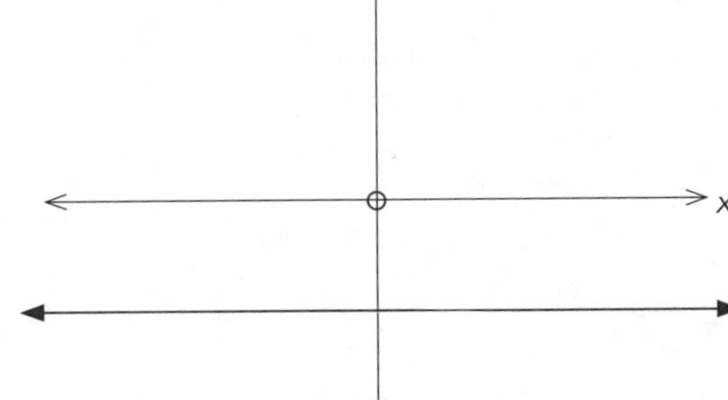

6

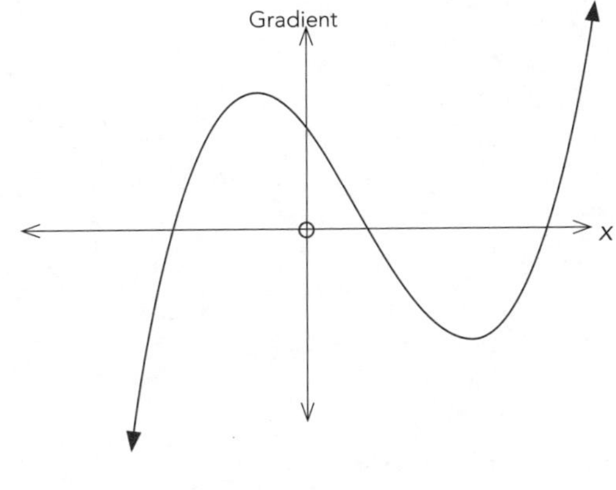

ISBN: 9780170354233

7

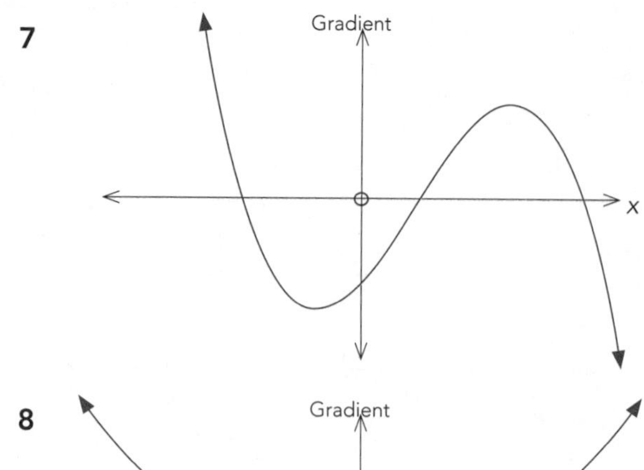

8

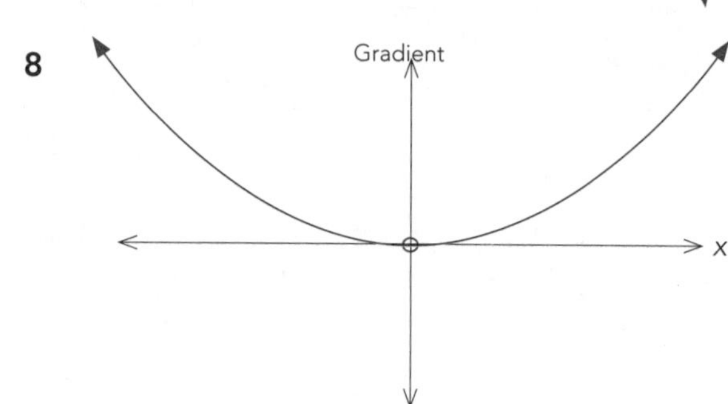

Differentiation (pp. 15–51)

Differentiating a polynomial (p. 16–17)

1 $\frac{dy}{dx} = 21x^2$
2 $f'(x) = 2x$
3 $\frac{dy}{dx} = 45x^4$
4 $f'(x) = 0$
5 $\frac{dy}{dx} = 23$
6 $f'(x) = 24x^7 + 5$
7 $\frac{dy}{dx} = 30x^4 + 4$
8 $f'(x) = -0.15$
9 $\frac{dy}{dx} = -2 + 22x$
10 $f'(x) = 3x^2 - 16x + 23$
11 $\frac{dy}{dx} = \frac{1}{2}$
12 $f'(x) = \frac{4}{5}x^3 + 2$
13 $\frac{dy}{dx} = -\frac{27}{10}x^2$
14 $f'(x) = 2x + \frac{1}{10}$
15 $\frac{dy}{dx} = 2 - 6x$
16 $f'(x) = -6x - 6$
17 $\frac{dy}{dx} = -\frac{1}{2}x^4$
18 $f'(x) = 0.01x + 0.004$
19 $\frac{dy}{dx} = -0.1$
20 $f'(x) = \frac{28}{10}x^3 - \frac{7}{10}$
21 $\frac{dy}{dx} = 2x^4 + 2$
22 $f'(x) = 3x^2 - 16x + 16$
23 $\frac{dy}{dx} = -16x + 22$
24 $\frac{dy}{dx} = 18x - 42$

Using a differentiated polynomial to calculate the gradient (given value for *x*) (p. 19)

1 3
2 -6
3 -1
4 -12
5 12. This is a straight line, so the gradient will be 12 anywhere along it.
6 15
7 -0.5
8 3
9 4
10 -0.25
11 23.75
12 -12

Using a differentiated polynomial to calculate the gradient (given value for *y*) (p. 21)

1 $x = -4 \longrightarrow m = -8$
$x = 4 \longrightarrow m = 8$
2 $x = 2 \longrightarrow m = 12$
3 $x = 2 \longrightarrow m = -8$
$x = 0 \longrightarrow m = -8$
$x = -2 \longrightarrow m = -8$
This is a straight line and the gradient is -8 anywhere along it.
4 $x = 3 \longrightarrow m = 6$
$x = -3 \longrightarrow m = -6$
5 $x = 0 \longrightarrow m = 5$
$x = 5 \longrightarrow m = -5$
6 $x = 7 \longrightarrow m = 14$
$x = -7 \longrightarrow m = -14$
7 $x = -3 \longrightarrow m = -5$
$x = 2 \longrightarrow m = 5$
8 $x = 0.5 \longrightarrow m = 7$
$x = -3 \longrightarrow m = -7$
9 $x = 6 \longrightarrow m = -12$
$x = -6 \longrightarrow m = 12$
10 $f(x) = 4 \longrightarrow m = 4$
$f(x) = -4 \longrightarrow m = -4$

Given the equation and coordinates of a point, find the equation of the tangent (p. 23)

1 $y = 6x - 9$
2 $f(x) = 13x - 4$
3 $y = 7x + 1$
4 $f(x) = -5x + 4$
5 $y = 7x - 15$
6 $y = x$
7 $x = 2 \longrightarrow m = 24$, $y = 0$, so $y = 24x - 48$
$x = -2 \longrightarrow m = -24$, $y = 0$, so $y = -24x - 48$
8 $y = 16$
9 $y = -6x + 28$
10 $y = -27x - 54$
11 $y = -5x + 1$
12 $y = 11x - 5$

Using a differentiated polynomial to locate points where the curve has a given gradient (p. 25)

1 (3, 9)
2 (2, 24)
3 (2, -5)
4 (2, -3)
5 (-1, 5)
6 (1, 3)

ISBN: 9780170354233

7 (1, 11⅔) and (-1, 10⅓)
8 (2, -16) and (-2, 16)
9 (3, -3.5) and (-3, 23.5)
10 (-4, 26 ⅓) and (4, -16⅓)
11 (1, 2) and (-1, -2)
12 (0, 0) and $(2, \frac{-4}{3})$

Putting it all together (pp. 26–27)

1 (-1, 14.5)
2 $y = -12$
3 (1, 7) and (-1, -5)
4 $m = -\frac{3}{2}$
5 $y = 8x - 16$ and $y = -8x - 16$
6 (-1, 6)
7 $y = -2x + 3$
8 $y = 2x - 8$
9 (2, 22) and (-2,-22)
10 m = -5.2
11 $y = -27x + 81$
12 $x = 0 \rightarrow m = 3$

Locating turning points and determining their nature (p. 30)

1 (4, -13), minimum
2 (-6, -36), minimum
3 (-3, 64), maximum
(3, -44), minimum
4 (-4, 17), maximum
(0, -15), minimum
5 (-5, -101), minimum
(1, 7), maximum

Finding where functions are increasing and decreasing (p. 32)

1 $x > 4$
2 $x < 6$
3 $x < -1$ and $x > 1$
4 $-4 < x < 0$
5 $-3 < x < 1$

1a: Rates of change (given value of x) (p. 34)

1 The rate of increase is 75 cm³/cm of side.
2 The stone is dropping at 30 m/s.
3 The area is increasing by 3π m² per m of radius.
4 The population is increasing at 10.8 animals per year.

1b: Rates of change (given value of y) (p. 35)

1 $x = 8$ cm $\rightarrow \frac{dV}{dx} = 192$ cm³ per cm
2 $t = 2.828$ s $\rightarrow = \frac{dH}{dt} = -56.568$ m per second

1c: Rates of change (given value of $\frac{dy}{dx}$) (p. 36)

1 $x = 4$ cm
2 After 2 seconds

Mixing it up (pp. 37–38)

1 Temperature is dropping at 0.35°C per hour.
2 $t = 3$ min $\rightarrow V = 27.5$ litres
3 $r = 5$ cm $\rightarrow \frac{dV}{dr} = 75\pi$
4 $r = 6$ cm
5 24 ice blocks per day
6 $L = 10$ cm
7 $w = 10 \rightarrow$ she is making 3 more cakes per week
8 Another 21 items

2 Optimisation (pp. 40–41)

1 Width = 2 m and maximum height is 2.5 m
2 Maximum height = 7.25 m
3 Maximum items sold is 533.5 (so 533) when $17,000 is spent on advertising
4 Maximum depth = 1.8 m
5 After 3 minutes
6 Maximum density is 1203 bacteria/mL when the nutrient given is 14.43 mg
7 Peaks after 20 years with 161 rabbits
8 $x = 4 \rightarrow V = 256$, which is the maximum volume
$x = 12 \rightarrow V = 0$, which is the minimum volume

3 Optimisation with related variables (pp. 44–51)

1 Pen is 12 m by 24 m and area is 288 m²
2 $x = 30$ cm $\rightarrow$ dimensions are 30 x 60 x 50 cm
Maximum surface area = 12,600 cm²
3 Each side is 19 cm and the area is 361 cm²
4 Short fences are 8 m
Length of enclosure = 24 m
Maximum area = 192 m²
5 Minimum $\rightarrow x = y = 7.5$
Show this is a minimum:
$x = 8 \rightarrow x^2 + y^2 = 113$
$x = 7.5 \rightarrow x^2 + y^2 = 112.5$
$x = 7 \rightarrow x^2 + y^2 = 113$
6 $x = 24$ cm $\rightarrow$ Volume = 0, so this is a minimum
$x = 8$ cm $\rightarrow$ Volume = 8192 cm³, which is the maximum. Dimensions are 32 x 32 x 8 cm.
7 $r = 1.1284$ cm, maximum volume = 9.0270 cm³
8 $r = 12$, $h = 6$, maximum volume = 2714 cm³

Anti-differentiation (pp. 52–66)

Anti-differentiating a polynomial (p. 54)

1 $y = 2x^4 + c$
2 $f(x) = \frac{1}{3}x^3 + c$
3 $y = -x^6 + c$
4 $f(x) = 10x + c$
5 $y = 11.5x^2 + c$
6 $f(x) = 3x^9 + 5x^2 + c$
7 $y = x^6 + 2x^2 - 2x + c$
8 $g(x) = 7x - 0.125x^2 + c$

ISBN: 9780170354233

9 $y = -8x - x^2 + 0.1x^3 + c$

10 $f(x) = \frac{1}{4}x^4 - \frac{8}{3}x^3 + 11x^2 - 4x + c$

Calculating c

1 Given point on original curve (pp. 56–57)

1	$y = -x^2 + 5$	2	$y = 4x^2 + 7x + 3$
3	$y = -x^2 + 2x + 2$	4	$g(x) = x^3 - 5x + 4$
5	$f(x) = x^2 + 6x + 9$	6	$y = -5x - 3$
7	$y = x^4 + 2x - 7$	8	$f(x) = 2x^3 - x^2 + 1$
9	$y = 9 - x^2 - 12x^3$	10	$h(x) = -2x^4 + 3x^2 - 1$

Challenges and applications (pp. 58–59)

1	$f(x) = x^2 - 4x + 1$	2	$y = x^2 - 6x + 13$
3	$y = x^3 - 3x - 2$	4	$y = x^3 - 6x^2 + 9x$
5	$f(x) = x^2 + 3x - 5$		
6	$g(x) = -0.25x^2 - 3x - 13$		
7	$h(x) = 2x^2 - 7x + 8$		

2 Given a point in a rate of change problem (pp. 60–62)

1 a $2900 - 52t + 0.2t^2$
  b 1940 L of diesel left

2 a $P(t) = 0.5t^2 - 0.004t^3 + 50$
  b 96 animals

3 a $V(t) = 12t^2 + 20t + 1000$
  b $V(10) = \$2400$

4 a $N = 300 - 5t - 2t^2$
  b 3 ice blocks left

5 a $V = 0.08r^3$
  b Weight is 17.28 g

6 a $V = 2t^2 - 0.1t + 11$
  b 809 L water

7 a $T(h) = 41 - 0.04t - 0.01t^2$
  b 39.6°C

3 Using graph of the gradient function to sketch the original curve (pp. 64–66)

1

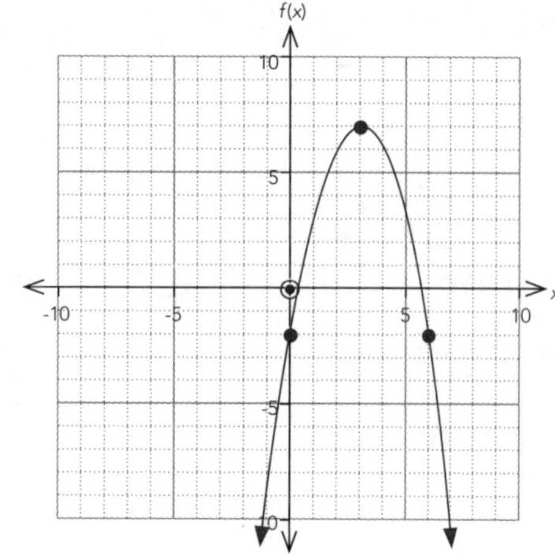

2

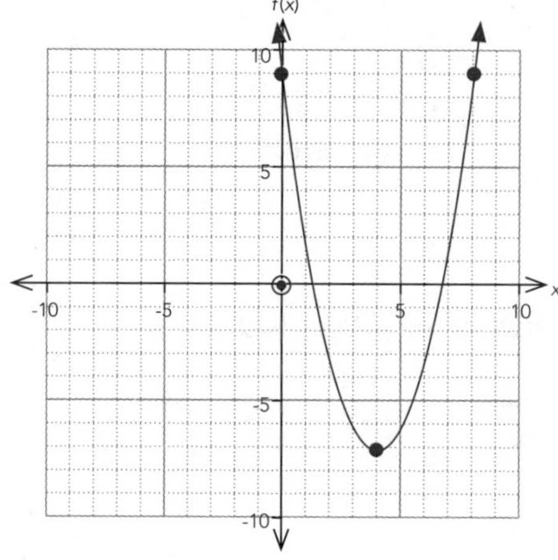

3

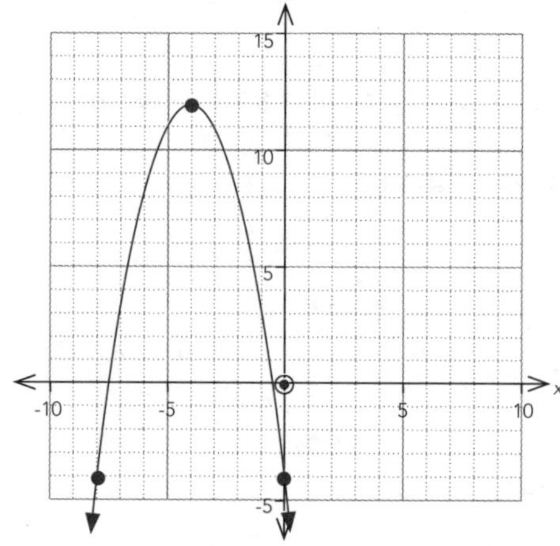

4

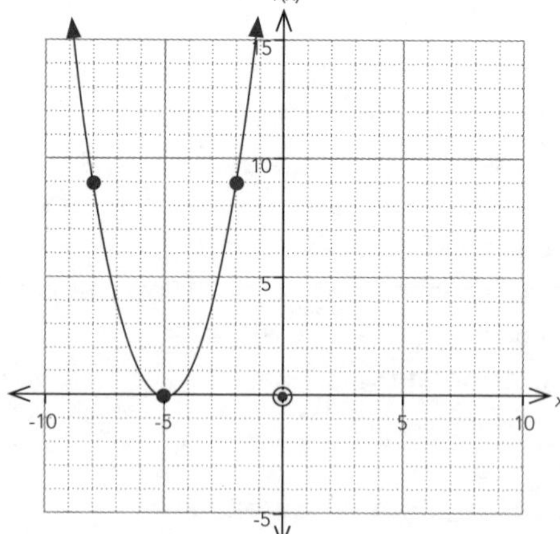

5

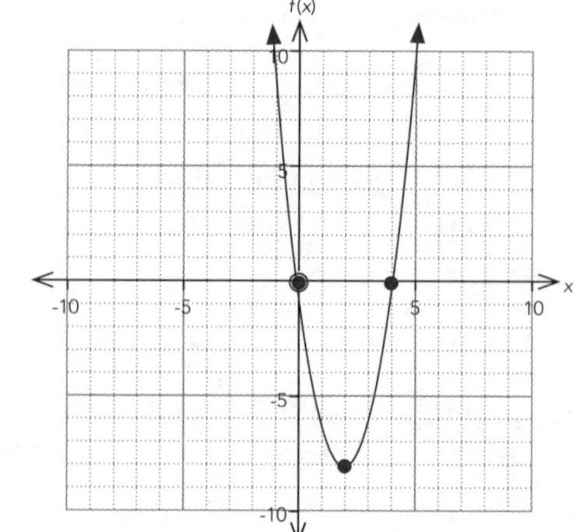

 ISBN: 9780170354233

6

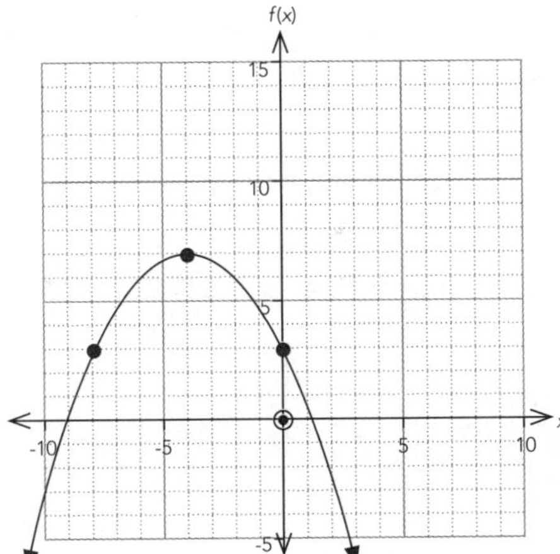

Kinematics (pp. 67–80)

Differentiation in kinematics (pp. 69–72)

1 **a** 2 m above the ground
b $h = 15$ m
c $v = 10$ m/s
d $a = -10$ m/s^2
e $h = 22$ m
f $t = 0.8$ s

2 **a** $s = 15.2$ m
b $v = 4.6$ m/s
c At $t = 15$ s
d $a = 0.4$ m/s^2

3 **a** 20 m/s
b Distance = 20 m
c Depth = $s = 44.10$ m

4 **a** $s = 7.11$ m
b $v = 6.67$ m/s
c $a = 2.67$ m/s^2
d After 6 seconds when it was 48 m from the station.
e $t = 18$ s
f After 12 s it was 96 m from the station.

5 **a** $s = 16$ m
b $v = 4$ m/s
c After 3 seconds
d $s = 18$ m
e -4 m/s^2. This means the bowl is slowing down by 4 m/s every second.
f Because the bowl stops after 3 seconds. However, the relationship means that after 3 seconds the bowl would start to move back towards Phoebe.

Anti-differentiation in kinematics

1a Anti-differentiating once to calculate c (given velocity, calculate distance) (pp. 74–75)

1 Height = 180 m
2 Height = 5.6 km
3 **a** 180 m
b After 14 seconds
c 196 m
4 Depth = 50.18 m
5 Depth = 16.94 m
6 **a** After 17.32 s
b Distance = 207.85 cm
7 Distance = 390 m

1b Anti-differentiating once to calculate c (given acceleration, calculate velocity) (pp. 76–77)

1 $v = 17.64$ m/s
2 $v = 10$ m/s
3 **a** Maximum height reached after 1.22 s
b $v = 2.2$ m/s
4 $v = 6.75$ m/s
5 $t = 1.9$ s

2 Anti-differentiating twice to calculate c and c′ (given acceleration, calculate distance) (pp. 79–80)

1 $s = 1080$ m
2 **a** time = 15 s
b distance = 225 m
3 $s = 900$ m
4 **a** $t = 13.66$ s
b $s = 328.7$ m
5 Spanner takes 2.45 s
6 $s = 133.\dot{3}$ m

Practice questions (pp. 81–90)

Practice question one (pp. 81–82)

a $f'(2) = 29$
b $g(x) = 5x - x^3 + 13$
c 22 m
d After 10 hours
e $-2 < x < 2$
f $y = -2x^3 + 6x^2 - 7$

Practice question two (pp. 83–84)

a $x = 5$
b Gradient = ±6
c $A = 4$, $h(x) = -x^2 + 4x - 1$
d $v = 3t + 6$, so $v = 24 \longrightarrow t = 6$ s
e $r = 6$, so $\frac{dV}{dr} = 144\pi$

f

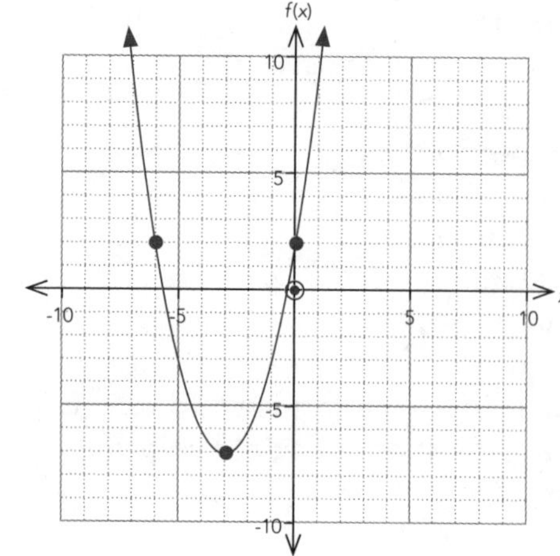

Practice question three (pp. 85–86)

a $f(x) = 5x - 2x^2 - 3$, so $x = -1 \longrightarrow y = -10$

b -37, so the population is reducing by 37 birds per year

c $y = -11x + 12$

d $h(x) = -x^2 + 5x - 7$

e $s = 2t - 0.005t^2 \longrightarrow s(120) = 168$ m

f $2x + y = 15$

Sum $= 5x^2 - 60x + 225 = 0 \longrightarrow x = 6, y = 3$

Practice question four (pp. 87–88)

a Check with your teacher

b (2.4, -25.8)

c $9700

d Show that $\frac{dH}{dx} = 0 \longrightarrow x = 6, y = 3$

Then $x = 9 \longrightarrow h = 2.98$

$x = 10 \longrightarrow h = 3$

$x = 11 \longrightarrow h = 2.98$

So maximum is where $x = 10$ m.

(Or alternative method.)

e $f(x) = -2x^3 + 9x + 3$ so $f(-1) = -4$

f $v = 1.6t - \frac{1}{40}t^2$

$s = 0.8t^2 - \frac{1}{120}t^3$

$s(20) = 253.3$ m

Practice question five (pp. 89–90)

a

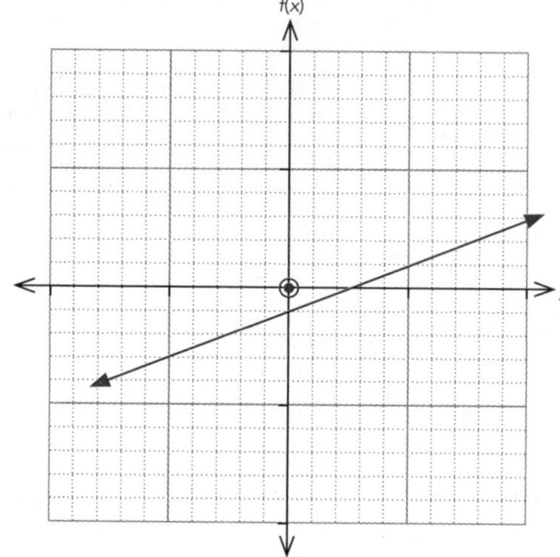

b $f(x) = 0.25x^2 - 5x + 6$

c $1 < x < 5$

d $f'(v) = -0.4 + 0.02v = 0$

$f = \frac{0.4}{0.02}$

$f = 20$

$f'(19) = -0.02$

$f'(20) = 0.02$

$\therefore$ a minimum occurs where $v = 20$

(or equivalent answer)

e 5 seconds

f Volume = $1365.3\,\pi$ cm^3

ISBN: 9780170354233